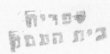

AMERICAN JEWS IN ISRAEL

AMERICAN JEWS IN ISRAEL

HAROLD R. ISAACS

THE JOHN DAY COMPANY

NEW YORK

Library of Congress Catalogue Card Number: 66-22934

PRINTED IN THE UNITED STATES OF AMERICA
BY AMERICAN BOOK–STRATFORD PRESS, INC.

A Study from the Center for International Studies,
Massachusetts Institute of Technology

What mean ye, that ye use this proverb concerning the land of Israel, saying, The fathers have eaten sour grapes, and the children's teeth are set on edge? As I live, saith the Lord God, ye shall not have occasion any more to use this proverb in Israel. Behold, all souls are mine; as the soul of the father, so also the soul of the son is mine. . . .

EZEKIEL, 18:1–4

Contents

Prefatory Note   5

1. *Introduction:* The Study of Group Identity and Political Change   15

2. Numbers   42

3. Name To Go By: The "Anglo-Saxons"   54

4. Why They Came   70

5. Problems of Living   92

6. Being "Americans"   104

7. Being "Jews"   123

8. Becoming "Israelis"   165

   Index   247

Prefatory Note

This report on American Jews living in Israel is one of a series of exploratory case studies of the interaction of group identity and political change. It is based on interviews conducted in 1963 with about fifty American settlers and would-be settlers in Israel. It examines in some detail a major dilemma of identity as it emerged from these interviews, a difficult problem of choice of nationality. This dilemma was created in part by the fact that under existing American laws, it was impossible for these Americans to participate fully in Israeli life without jeopardizing or forfeiting their American citizenship. They could not, for example, legally vote in Israeli elections or serve in the Israeli armed forces unless they were willing to forego their American citizenship and become citizens of Israel. Since most of these Americans (their total number is something over 10,000) were unwilling to become Israelis at the cost of giving up their legal status as Americans, this became and remained for many of them a

5

painfully unresolved problem of their lives as settlers in Israel.

On May 29, 1967, the United States Supreme Court handed down a ruling which largely relieved these Americans of the legal or more formal aspect of their national identity dilemma. In a case which involved an American citizen whose citizenship had been revoked because he had voted in an Israeli election, the court ruled that Congress did not have the power to pass laws depriving Americans of their nationality without their consent. This ruling reversed a number of previous decisions and apparently threw out as unconstitutional all the laws passed by Congress that provided for withdrawal of citizenship from Americans in various prescribed circumstances. Just how far this decision went was not quite clear. Only further test will show, for example, whether Americans now can become citizens of another country without ceasing to be citizens of the United States, a practice of dual citizenship freely allowed by many other countries. But even as it stood, the new court ruling came as an act of rescue for many Americans in Israel and it could hardly have come at a more dramatic moment.

Israel was that very day near the crest of the mortal crisis that had begun with threatening moves by Egypt in mid-May and ended with Israel's stunningly swift victory over the combined forces of all its Arab neighbors in the first week of June. It was a time when many of these Americans had reason to feel more painfully than ever the cost of the ambivalence that kept them out of the armed forces mobilized to preserve Israel's existence. Whatever the strength of their feelings, they could not share unreservedly as full-fledged Israelis in the resurgence of Israeli national emotions brought on by the new threat to Israel's survival. It was obvious that when the tide of this crisis receded, the reappearing shape of things would be both much the same and much altered, strategically, politically, emotionally. Whatever the nature of the relative "peace" these events could now produce, triumphant Israeli nationalism, flushed with armed victory, had freshened its aura and achieved a heightened dominance. Its impact was going to be felt not only on the balance of power in the whole region and on the politics of both Arab countries and Israel, but also on the emotions and behavior of every individual in this drama from the most visible to the most obscure. The new surge of Jewish national feeling and identity produced by this crisis was shared not only by Jews in Israel but by Jews everywhere. It cut across divisions and differences of every kind. The emotional identification with Israel, stretched thin in many respects by the "normalization" process, was strongly reestablished. If this was true to a degree of the great mass of American Jews in America, the effect was undoubtedly all the greater on the small group of American Jews living in Israel who are the subjects of the present report.

In the pages that follow, a great many of these latter Americans appear as individuals caught in a complicated set of push-and-pull pressures which had prevented them—in some cases for many years—from resolving their problem of national identity. They were pulled strongly enough by Israel to cause them to migrate from America and seek to make their lives in the new Jewish state. But most of them clung strongly enough to America to find it impossible to become Israelis in the full sense of an unqualified acceptance of Israeli nationality. The events of May–June 1967 could hardly have failed to affect these conflicting pulls, to reinforce the pull from Israel, with its proud and forceful reassertion of its national presence and armed power, and to weaken the counter-pull from America, which could have appeared to them in this moment of crisis to be corroded by the cross-pressures of the power struggle with Russia, ready to dilute its moral commitments, hesitant to redeem pledges to Israel far more explicit than those being honored at such cost in Vietnam, saved from a shameful betrayal only by the single-handed success of Israeli arms against the Arab foe. Whether this crisis by itself would have brought any or many of these Americans to resolve this ambivalence we do not know and now may never know, for the May 29 decision of the United States Supreme Court has apparently removed most or all of the legal restraints which previously had made their dilemma so explicit and so formal. Now they may indeed be able at last to enjoy the best of both their worlds. If the new decision means that they can now freely meet all the same obligations incurred by Israeli citizens while remaining American citizens, that will be, for many of them, quite enough. If on further clarification it develops that they can actually become citizens of Israel while remaining citizens of the United States, it will be the consummation most of them have devoutly wished could somehow come to pass. Their unique personal crisis of national identity will have been resolved, not by them or their own choice, to be sure, but by larger forces and pressures working around and upon them. This, with drama to spare, is a striking example of the impact of political change on group identity.

When these events at the end of May and early June 1967 were unfolding, this book was about to go to press. What the United States Supreme Court decision of May 29, 1967, does to this account essentially is to change its tense. It makes it all the sharper as a vignette illustrating a larger subject. That subject is the impact of political change on group identity. This is by definition a subject in motion, a process taking place, a transformation occurring in a host of different ways to many different kinds of people. Every one of the case studies in this series has moved and shifted and been affected by events even as I sought out its details, much less set down and published what I learned. It is precisely this process of change that I have been trying to catch and hold for a moment's scrutiny, like a frame of a motion-picture film stopped for a longer look.

Were this work still being written, I would have the task of incorporating the further outcomes which events have provided for it. Since it was already in type, however, I am glad to let it stand as it is. I have only to ask the reader to keep in mind that where it refers to the citizenship dilemma suffered by these Americans in Israel, the tense is no longer present but past. Where practicable, I have inserted footnote reminders to this effect. This remains a case study in group identity, not a topical report, or a history, or a treatment of the larger context in which its subjects move. It is a small, exploratory study, moreover, which opens a subject that is far from closed. On its own terms I am sure it is subject to all kinds of challenge, question and elaboration, and I trust it may receive all these in good measure and that the continuing experience of Americans in Israel will find chroniclers who will keep them in view in their own small corner of the larger scene. Insofar as this work contributes to the continuing study of the nature of group identity and its interaction with political change, it will have served its essential purpose. I can only hope that in addition to serving this larger function, it retains its own intrinsic interest for the reader who comes to it for its own sake.

For help of many different kinds during the course of this inquiry, for courtesy and hospitality, and most of all for generous cooperation and patience, I owe grateful thanks to a great many people. I owe most to those who took part in our interviews and shared their experience with us. For great assistance of a most practical kind, I have special acknowledgments to make to Murray Greenfield, then executive director of the Association of Americans and Canadians in Israel, and David Breslau of Hillel, in Jerusalem, more recently president of the Association. For helping us to enlarge our view of much in Israel beyond the immediate scope of our inquiry, I have to thank our old friends Michael and Patricia Gurevitch. Not one of these individuals can bear any responsibility for how I have understood and used what they helped me to learn. I am sure that many of them would view or interpret these experiences differently, and indeed several have written to tell me so. This is only natural. My concern is that the facts are straight, that the most rigorous justice has been done to each person's account, that all quotations are faithfully rendered, that respect for each one's integrity and privacy has been fully and scrupulously maintained.

For reading all or parts of this report at various stages, for corrections, comments, criticisms, and challenges, I owe great thanks to David Breslau, Moshe Kerem of Gesher Haziv, Aaron Antonovsky of the Institute of Social Research in Jerusalem, Prof. Simon Herman of Hebrew University, Daniel Shimshoni, Prof. Ben Halpern of Brandeis University, Prof. Alex

Weingrod, also of Brandeis, Dr. Ernest Stock of the Jacob Hiatt Institute in Jerusalem, Rabbi Ira Eisenstein of New York, Dr. M. J. Dulfano of Newton, Mass., and my colleague Prof. Leonard J. Fein of M.I.T. For turning my thoughts in the direction of this inquiry in the first place, for reading the results, for much helpful comment and profitable conversation, I have special thanks also to offer to Prof. Jacob Neusner of Dartmouth College. Every one of these individuals saved me from making not a few small errors and virtually all of them did what they could to save me from making what they sometimes saw as much larger errors of judgment or interpretation. Wherever I accepted their counsel, I am sure I greatly improved my text. Where I have stubbornly persisted, I may simply have compounded my errors, if such they be, but this makes them all the more clearly mine. I have done everything I could to insure that I alone am responsible for any part of this report which anyone may think wrong or wrong-headed.

For the sponsorship which has enabled me to pursue the whole series of studies of which this is part, I have continuing acknowledgment to make to the Center for International Studies at M.I.T. and to the National Institute of Mental Health for the grant which has specifically supported this work. For research and secretarial assistance at various stages, I have to thank Mrs. Deirdre Bonifaz, Mrs. Laura Farnsworth, and Mrs. Margot Krebs.

Beyond acknowledgment lies what I have continued to share with Viola R. Isaacs, who joined indispensably in the making of this inquiry, was involved in many of the interviews, transcribed all the notes, mulled and argued the meaning of each encounter and each day's exposures, and by her constant presence once more made work and travel what it has always been when we have done it together, fun.

H.R.I.

Cambridge, Massachusetts
June 11, 1967

A considerable portion of the material in this report appeared in The New Yorker.

1. Introduction: The Study of Group Identity and Political Change

Several years ago I published an account of what I had learned about the experience of a small number of American Negroes I had met in several countries of West Africa during the summer of 1960.* One of the many lively reactions produced by that report was a letter from a young American Jewish scholar who said that the experiences and emotions described by many of these American Negroes in West Africa were in many ways similar to those shared by many American Jews, including himself, who had gone to Israel, and he urged me to go to Israel to discover this for myself. In pursuit of my continuing studies of the interaction of group identity and political change, in 1963 I did go

* This account appeared originally under the title "Back to Africa" in *The New Yorker*, May 13, 1961, and was later included in a book, *The New World of Negro Americans*, The John Day Company, New York, 1963.

15

to Israel where this interaction is taking place in a unique way among all the Jews who now live there and especially among the American Jews about whom I went particularly to learn. I found, despite obvious great differences of kind, scope, scale, and circumstance, that many of these American Jews in Israel did indeed have something in common with the American Negroes I had met earlier in West Africa. In both cases they were people who felt themselves to be "outsiders" in the American society and out of this common feeling had gone off to Africa or to Israel to find ways of belonging among their own kind, to become "insiders" as *Negroes* or as *Jews*. What they most commonly found instead, in both instances, was that they remained "outsiders" as *Americans*. This was only one of the several threads linking these two inquiries, for I was interested not only in each individual experience and in each group for its own sake, but I was also trying to learn something about the nature of group identity in general and of the American group identity in particular. Of the Negro experience in Africa, I had written:

> . . . Practically all the American Negroes I met in West Africa had come to the ancestral continent . . . looking for freedom from racism and prejudice, or at least for a racial situation that counted them in instead of out—that provided solace and a sense of identity in a world in which everyone was black. They had also looked for a chance to share in the new pride of achieve-

ment stemming from the black man's reassertion of himself and his African personality. In West Africa, in a small way and for a short time, the Negro pilgrim can find some of this. But it does not last long—hardly past the first blush of the sensation of being in a place where the white man is not master. Almost invariably [he] finds himself not free at all, more than ever without solace and a sense of identity, fighting new patterns of prejudice and suffering the pangs of a new kind of outsiderness. He had thought he was alien in America, but he discovers that he is more alien in Africa. Whether he likes it or not he is American, and in Africa he becomes an American in exile.

Coming back to comment on my account after several years of his own much more extensive experience in Africa, Charles J. Patterson, himself a Negro, writing in one of his reports for the Institute of Current World Affairs* said that most of the American Negroes he had met in Africa had "not come as pilgrims" and did not have "a doomed expectation of belonging" but instead derived their greatest solace and satisfaction from discovering that they did indeed find a situation that "counted them in"—"but," he went on, "they have found it not among Africans but among their fellow Americans working in Africa." Patterson offered this observation in what he seemed to think was a contradiction, or at least a correction of my own, but I readily accept his conclusion as being the same as

---

* "Harold Isaacs Revisited," Institute of Current World Affairs, June, 1964.

mine. In his words: "For most Negro Americans, being in Africa does confirm their American identity." And he added: "It is a surprising and pleasant experience for Americans who heretofore have been first, foremost, and only Negroes."

Changing the great deal that has to be changed, this still suggests much of the essence of what had also happened to many of the American Jews I interviewed in Israel, except that it was much less likely in their case to be a "surprising and pleasant experience." The differences, of course, are great. The number of American Negroes who have gone to Africa to live permanently is probably still countable only in the hundreds and chances are that most of them see themselves more as expatriates than as would-be immigrants. There is actually no counterpart for Negroes in Africa for the "homeland" that beckons Jews to Israel, no comparable ingathering of the lost children of any racial or national covenant. Though there has been some small recent growth of the nationalist and racialist groups that have long existed at the fringes of American Negro life, none of them has seriously advanced the idea of migration to Africa as the way to a better life for Negro Americans. The recent African emergence has spurred no revival among Negroes in America of the Garvey movement that called upon them to go "back to Africa" forty years ago when that continent was still part of Europe's empires. The great mass of Negroes, like the great mass of Jews in

America, remains committed to the idea of the good life based on their successful integration in the American society as Americans. Only a few individuals have felt "pushed" or "pulled" enough to choose the path of migration, many fewer Negroes than Jews in this case. Only when compared to the number of migrating Negroes can the number of migrating Jews seem large, some hundreds compared to some thousands, but the flow of migrating Jews to Israel has nevertheless remained but a trickle, a net of "about 10,000," or not quite two-tenths of a percent of America's five and a half million Jews.

But these are Jews who do go as would-be migrants, who do want to make new lives for themselves on a permanent basis in Israel, and do have that "expectation of belonging." They go to Israel to "belong," to become "insiders"—"to see how it is," in the words of one of them, "not to be always on the periphery"—and this is where their painful confusion begins, where they begin to find how difficult it is for this to come about. Some plunge more deeply into the new life than others, but the great majority find that they are unable to commit themselves to full participation in it. They remain at its outer margins and they do this, moreover, not only because of circumstances or conditions they find in Israel but also because of blocks that come up within themselves. These go far beyond any of the expectable difficulties of adjustment in a new country among many strangers and beyond the material difficulties of existence, though these are not negligible matters. They may have to do in many cases, again, with purely personal limitations and problems. But for many they also have to do with deeply imbedded values and attachments, perceptions of what is good and what is not, of social, political, and even—or sometimes especially—religious values. In a peculiarly dramatic and painful way, this also becomes even a formal and symbolic matter; the great majority do not legally become Israelis but remain American citizens. The effect is that individuals who had come precisely for the high purpose of sharing in the life of the new nation of Jews end up refusing to embrace the new Jewish nationality. People who left one country in order to be able to participate more fully in another bar themselves from taking part in the politics or serving in the armed forces of the country in whose inside they had said they wanted to belong. The painfully deep gap this opens between professed goal and actual behavior is bridged at various levels by a great variety of rationalizations. The issue means, or is said to mean, different things to different people, but it clearly does mean, at best, that many Americans in Israel live on half-loaves. "Make no mistake about it," one of them said to me, "every American here carries his private agony around with him." Among the many kinds of confusion about identity that haunt Jews in Israel today, the American confusion is unique and uniquely troubled. This comes out of far more than the exclusiveness of the American law that so unfeelingly denies them the cake-eating, cake-having status of dual citizenship; it comes out of the uniquenesses of their identity as Americans. This is the major fact I learned about American Jews in Israel and its details form the main substance of this report.

Before going on, let me here offer some necessary indications of the basis for what I have to report on these matters, presenting first, as briefly as I can, the framework in which I place them.

I have been trying for some years now to learn something about the impact of political change on the group identities of individuals caught up in the great shifts and transformations of our times. I have been examining this experience in a number of different settings beginning with a study of changing American perceptions of China and India, continuing with a report on the experiences of a group of college-age Americans entering upon their first encounter with Africa and Africans, an extended study of the impact of world political change and especially the African emergence on Negroes in America. These were followed by a series of briefer exploratory case studies of which the first to appear was a report on how educated former Untouchables have been faring in India in the new circumstances created by Indian independence. The present report on American Jews trying to live as

Israelis in Israel is the next of these studies and will be followed in one form or another by reports of what I learned during this same series of inquiries about Chinese trying to become Malaysians in Malaysia, post-colonial Filipinos in the process of defining what it now means to be Filipino, and post-imperial Japanese re-creating a concept of the Japanese nation to replace the one that was destroyed by defeat in the Great Pacific War. In each of these cases, I have been concerned with the interaction between group identity and political change, the wrenching shifts in self-definition and relationship caused by the great overturn of the power systems that had been established during the epoch of Western white world dominance. This has led me into some of the more obscure inwardnesses of the process of social change as it is experienced by individuals, especially by those whose lives have been all or most largely lived in these past twenty-five years or so since the most dramatic of these changes began to come to pass. It has required me to try to define what I mean by basic group identity and to learn something about how it functions and what tasks it performs.

By basic group identity, I mean the ready-made set of identifications which every individual shares with others from the moment of his birth. These mostly lie just beyond what he acquires in his genes and whatever it is that comes by osmosis through the parental membrane and gives each new personality the original shape of its unique self. The elements of his group identity come to the person by virtue of where, when, and to whom he is born. They are what he begins to breathe in from his first breath. They are his shared holdings, the social features, or what Erik Erikson has called the "shared samenesses" that enter into the makeup of his ego identity. No small store of acquisitions awaits each newborn babe: his ethnic being, family and group name; color and physical characteristics; the history and origins of the group into which he is born, its whole culture-past providing him, among other things, with his language, religion, arts, modes and styles of life, inherited value system; his nationality or other condition of national or tribal awareness; and finally the total structure of his culture-present, with all its intersecting, concentric, and multiple enlargements, the social-economic threshold of the family through which he enters life, the geography, politics, and economics of the country of his birth, and all the impinging circumstances of his time. These are all basically the ingredients of the common culture in which he comes as an individual to share.

The function of this basic group identity is to provide an individual with a supporting measure of self-acceptance, self-pride, self-esteem. Some people can derive a sufficient self-esteem out of the stuff of their individual personalities, above, beyond, or often despite, the character or situation of their group. Others depend heavily on their group identity to supply what their own individualities may deny them. Most people need all they can get from both sources. Many men find this need satisfied in one or more of the many other multiple group identities they acquire in the course of their lives, as members of that team, club, school, military outfit, occupation, business or professional group, or whatever. But these secondary sources of self-esteem are adequate only where the conditions created by the basic group identity do not get in the way. This can occur up to a point in a ghetto situation, for example, or wherever a similarly tight homogeneity exists. But such protective walls around a shared identity have rarely stood long and none forever—even the great Wall of China was finally battered down. Relationship and interaction with other groups govern in the lives of most people, even in historic periods we think of as "stable," and it is here where the elements of basic group identity become the essential determinants of group self-esteem. This takes place at many different levels and in many different ways, and is influenced by many different conditions. I am suggesting that chief, and probably decisive, among these are the *political conditions,* i.e., the conditions of power in which the group identity is held. How dominant or how dominated is the group to which the individual belongs, and how, therefore, is he able to bear himself in relation to others? This, I think, is the cardinal question and it is essentially a question of politics or power. Like health or money, group identity presents no problem when it is an assured given, when the self-acceptance it generates is an unquestioned premise of life. It is only when it is failing to give a man an acceptable basis for pride in himself—or worse, forcing him into a pattern of self-rejection—that it becomes a problem and, sooner or later, a matter of crisis. This is precisely the point at which group identity and politics meet. It is the starting point of much notable history, of many notable lives. This has been a critical point at all times, but never more so than in a time like the present when all power systems are changing, all group relationships being revised, and all group identities being forced to rearrange themselves to meet the transforming circumstances.

This is the current condition of all sorts and kinds of men and it is this difficult and complicated process of changing identity patterns that I have been trying to examine in a variety of settings. My own studies have touched now on six groups, including racial, caste, and national minorities of varying sizes in the United States, Israel, India and Malaya, and segments of majority groups in the Philippines and Japan. But one can look in almost any direction for other examples: post-isolationist Americans, post-imperial Englishmen, post-colonial Africans, post-Hitler Germans, post-Stalin Russians, neo-imperial Chinese, or even post-imperial-would-be-neo-imperial Gaullist Frenchmen. The world is full of changing orders of things and no one is exempt from the turmoil, be he Eskimo

or Afrikaner, Fiji Islander or French Canadian,
American Confederate or Hausa tribesman. No one's
group identity stands intact, each is going through its
unique experience, each with its unique character
which one can seek to discover and to sort out. I have
attempted to examine this rearrangement of the elements of group identity by identifying the separate
parts and trying to discover how they fit together, how
they have been wrenched apart, how they are being
put together again, to see what lies at the core and what
at the edges, to see, if one can, how group identities are
being reshaped to meet the new demands and to satisfy
the new needs created by political change. My outline
or description of the makeup of group identity is still
crude and incomplete, but every one of these elements
has come sharply alive to the touch in every case I have
studied. If it is not yet an adequate description, it has
proved to be a most useful tool of inquiry, opening up
many new views of the changing ways in which people
are seeing themselves in these miasmic times.

The simple matter of *name*, to begin with, whether
the name of individuals or of groups, is probably the
most elementary of all symbols of identity. Yet quite by
itself it usually carries a great freight of meaning and
dramatically illustrates the crisis or problem in view. It
seldom is itself the heart of the matter but it often
points directly to where that heart can be found. Each
of my studies has included a chapter called "A Name
To Go By," dealing with the changing weights and

measures of the terms "Negro" and "colored" and the word "black" among Negro Americans, the burdens of shame and pollution carried by group and individual names among Indian ex-Untouchables, and, in the present work, the new pools of meaning forming around the terms "Jew" and "Israeli," the use of "Anglo-Saxon" and some of the other terminological curiosities that turn up so bountifully now in Israel. In other cases there will be something to be said about the history and usages of "Indio" and "Filipino" in the Philippines, and, indeed, about the name "Philippines" itself. There is at least a footnote to be included, in the case of the Japanese, about the use of the terms "Nihon" and "Nippon" as the country's name. In the recent great multiplication of nation-states in the world, the reappearance of long-submerged names —e.g. Viet Nam, Ghana, Mali, Zambia—reopens long-buried veins of identification with the past and reflects the rearrangement of complex patterns of self-rejection and self-pride that are implicit in the changed patterns of power.

The *nation* is almost universally a strong focal area in the makeup of a person's group identity. It appears at varying levels and in different situations as matters of nationality, nationalism, or some other measure of national consciousness. Political upheavals of recent decades made "stateless" or "displaced" persons out of millions of people who suddenly discovered, as Hannah Arendt has pointed out, that nationality had be-

come almost the only link between an individual and
the rest of humanity, and that to be without it was to
be cut off from all other people, indeed, often from life
itself. In addition to stateless people in a world of
multiplying states, we also now have people, like the
Chinese in Malaysia or Indonesia, whose access to
nationality in those countries has abruptly become a
central problem of their existence. In Israel, of course,
the reshaping of the Jewish experience in new national
terms is the very essence of the creation of the new
Israeli identity, raising a host of new questions about
the age-old problems of the nature of the Jewish identity. To the American Jews in Israel who are the
subjects of the present study, the matter of their
nationality as Americans or as Israelis becomes the
focal center of their own peculiar group identity problem. The drives of nationalism have been responsible
for the most sweeping of the political changes of our
era. The achievement of new nationhood is the most
visible group identity change of all in the world today;
some 70 new nations have been carved out of the ex-
empires of Europe in Asia and Africa. In most of them
the first task of the new men of power is actually to
create new national identities where none existed before, to provide a new sense of an enlarged community
that their fragmented peoples will recognize and accept. In many cases, these new nations are made up of
uncoalesced and often mutually hostile racial, tribal,
regional, and linguistic groupings. This will be the

source of turbulent conflict for a long time to come, even as it was—indeed still is—in much of Europe where French nationalism (in its superannuated Gaullist form) and German nationalism are still potent forces and where smaller barely stoked nationalist fires still burn among some groups of people all the way from Wales to Belgium to the Ukraine. Other kinds of national consciousness figure centrally but in different ways—in Germany and Japan, for example—where a new young adult generation needs to re-create the nation as an expression of group existence in a form morally more acceptable or tolerable than the nations which shaped their fathers. In all older states, indeed, the sense of nationhood has become the object of new gropings for self-definition in a world that is seeking but cannot find the way to some larger and saner kind of coherence.

Much less marginal in the makeup of group identity and more glandular than most degrees of national consciousness is the matter of *color and physical characteristics*. There is much about this matter that we know now better than we did, and much we still do not know at all. Color and physical characteristics are the obvious symbols of what has been called "race"; and "race," as we all know, has served all kinds of men as the basis of their self-esteem or their lack of it, and has occupied a central place in much of the human story. Our behavior in this respect still commonly ignores what is scientifically known now about "race." Skin color and physical characteristics still dominate the group identities of some men, black men in America and Africa whose blackness became the burden a white-dominated world placed upon them, and some white men, as in South Africa or Mississippi, for whom the element of "whiteness" remains the paramount element in life and whose present group identity crisis revolves around the maintenance of their myths about it. But this is hardly only a matter that lies between "blackness" and "whiteness." It appears with varying intensities along the entire color spectrum, among all shades of men who have attached values to "lightness" and "darkness" in almost every culture and place. These were submerged for a long time in the common subordination of all so-called "non-whites" to the so-called "whites." But now, when that power has been rediffused among the "non-whites" and the mantling mythology of white supremacy has been so largely pulled away, these older designs come again into view. We become aware of the many ways in which people who writhed under the superiority patterns of the "whites" now apply similarly based (and similarly baseless) superiority patterns of their own to the many shades of color differences among themselves. This is to be seen in India, in the Philippines, in North Africa, indeed just about everywhere. It is still the simplest thing for the new men of power to blame this on the legacy of Western white dominance, but this easy explanation does not always withstand a harder look. In any case, it is clear that in all its varieties and with all its sources, feeling about color and physical character- istics figures in a key way in every group identity. It is more major in some than in others, but it is never minor.

Inclusive of name, nation, and "race," and perhaps most crucial of all as a source of self-pride or the lack of it, is the nature of a man's *history and origins,* the whole culture-past out of which he comes, the sources of his myths, his language, his religion, his professed values, his art, the sum of continuity with the past which contributes its own peculiar quality of meaning- fulness to the individual life. The mix of it plainly varies greatly from group to group, different people using it in widely different ways and with different effect. The element of culture-past is plainly the key element in the remarkable survival of the Jews as a group, even though Jews disagree widely on how to understand what their past means to them now. In the case of the American Jews in Israel, it is the overlay of their history as Americans on their history as Jews that in large measure shapes their peculiar dilemma as would-be Israelis. In quite different ways, it is from their culture-past that both the Chinese and the In- dians, unlike peoples with very different histories, have extracted the self-satisfaction and pride which their other circumstances, especially in the last century or so, have so often denied them. In some quite narrowly defined groups, the whole stock of self-pride is some times supplied by group identities centered on the accident of descent itself, as among Brahmins in India who argue, of course, that *their* descent is no accident, or among any of the hereditary nobilities of Europe or Asia, or their American equivalents such as the descendants of the Mayflower company or the Daughters of the American Revolution. Individuals in these cases use some ancestral distinction to give content to lives that can otherwise be threateningly empty. Contrast these examples with that of the African, one of whose main problems of re-emergence is often the rediscovery and reassertion of *his* history, of his continuity through more than sheer survival, his possession of a past from which he can reclaim the legacies of pride that the white world, in the main, denied him through the long era of his submergence. Or consider the contrary example I have already cited, of the ex-Untouchable in India who wants to blot out his known past in order to give his children a fresh identity from which they can begin to derive some elementary self-respect.

There is no end to the particulars with which this outline can be filled, but perhaps we have carried them far enough here into the complexities of our culture-present to illustrate both the nature of group identity and its linkages with political change. It is obviously not enough, however, to identify these elements and arrange them in neat boxes, giving a speciously regular appearance to what is actually a confused splatter. No mind, no personality, no individual or group identity ever looks like a set of neat boxes. It is much more likely to look at first glance like a canvas produced by one of those paint-bucket-throwing artists who have mirrored for us what it is like to surrender to utter haplessness. Perhaps, if we stay with this metaphor, it may be more like a painting by Jackson Pollock whose whirls and whorls so often elusively are trying to mean something and where some quality of shape and color becomes somehow salient. But I do not think the vagueness and confusion are in fact quite so form-less. In my own mind I picture group identity as looking more like a cell of living matter with a sprawl-ingly irregular shape. It is part of a cluster of cells making up the ego identity, sharing elements and com-mon membranes with that other elusive quarry, the individual "personality." In it, floating or darting about, are specks, and flecks, bits and pieces, big shapes, little shapes, intersecting each other or hanging loose or clinging to one another, some out at the margins, some nearer the middle, some in wide orbits around the edges, some more narrowly moving deeper inside, but each one impinging upon, drawn to or repelled by a nuclear core that exerts its gravity upon them all and fixes the shape and content of the mes-sages that go out along the tiny meshes of the nervous system. The arrangement and mutual relationship of these elements differ from cell to cell and the nature of the nuclear core differs not only from cell to cell but can change within any one cell, all of these interactions having a fluid character and subject to alteration under the pressure of conditions that come in upon them from the outside. I think it is in these inwardnesses of group identity where we can learn more than we know now about the interactions of the individual, his group, and the larger politics of his time and place and more, therefore, about the nature of our common contemporary experience. There are a thousand questions here needing answers, hosts of subjects waiting their authors.

All this will, I hope, eventually acquire some fuller and more coherent form as I put together all the elements that emerge from these various studies. What I offer in these pages meanwhile is an interim report, some partial and incomplete illustrations of a particular case. I offer it in this form because I think each example commands its own interest, each group, indeed each individual experience, throwing its flicker of illumination on the great and tangled process of change through which we are all passing and in which, like it or not, we all share.

The Jews in Israel present a peculiarly dramatic example of this interaction between group identity and political change. They are trying to solve in the most explicitly political way the problems of marginality and outsiderness which dominated the Jewish experience for so long and the hostility and rejection which came to their ultimate climax in the Hitlerian holocaust. The re-establishment of Israel as a Jewish

state after an interval of some 2,000 years is an attempt
by some Jews not only to find ground on which to
defend themselves against Gentile hostility but also to
establish a national sum for their many parts. In this
new setting all the elements of the Jewish identity
come up not merely for redefinition or revision but for
re-creation, for all the Jews coming to Israel from all
parts of the world bring with them all their many
varieties of "Jewishness," reflecting all the many different kinds of cultural and physical identities acquired
from centuries of living among so many different kinds
of people. In Israel the question of questions becomes:
Who and what is a Jew? It is a question wrapped up
into a great swirl of cloudy confusion, unhelped by any
light at night, and it involves in some way for every
Jew some crucial decisions he must make for himself.
Its complexities touch upon every aspect of the past
and present of Jewish experience and raise all kinds of
formidably arguable questions about its meanings.
These are the specters that now haunt all Jews everywhere, Jews in Israel, Jews in America, and—the subjects of our immediate scrutiny—those American Jews
who have chosen to try to confront these great riddles
not in America but in Israel.

The material in these pages is based mainly on what
I learned in interviews conducted early in 1963 with
some 50 American Jews in Israel. I say "some 50"

because there were three group interviews (with a
roomful of parents on one kibbutz, a group of young
American one-year recruits on another, and a group of
American students at a language school in Jerusalem)
and if I counted them all as individuals, the total
would be greater. The ages of those I interviewed
ranged from the teens to the sixties and some 15 were
women. The panel of individuals included 22 kibbutzniks (on four kibbutzim, two each of the politically
distinct kibbutz federations linked to Mapai, the main
government party, and Mapam, long the left-wing op-
position party) and 22 city dwellers (including government servants, teachers and other professionals of
various kinds, and three businessmen). In addition
there were miscellaneous information-seeking interviews with Israeli government, Jewish Agency, and
American consular officials, officers of the British and
South African settler associations, and conversations
with Israelis of various backgrounds. These were my
direct sources and I must stress that they constitute a
group or a panel of informants and are not to be
confused with a sample, stratified or of any other kind,
nor is my inquiry to be confused with a sample survey.
The Association of Americans and Canadians in Israel
had been trying vainly for years, I was told by its
officers, to get such a survey made of its membership. It
probably reflects something about the "orphaned"
status of the group and perhaps even more about the
degree of interest in self-scrutiny among Americans in

Israel that the Association had not up to that time been able to attract funds or recruit any of its own locally available academic talent to carry out this modest little task. This is rather a pity, because much of the simpler kind of information one wants to know about such a group could perhaps best be gathered by this means. For my own part, this was not my task and sample-surveying is not my business. My own methods are more directly reportorial. I seek out a number of individuals involved in the experience, selecting them with a view to reaching a panel of informants as representative as possible of all the more important types and varieties concerned. In the present case, which was intended to be and is a limited and exploratory study, this is done to a very modest extent indeed. It is subject to many limitations and shortcomings, and I hope that my text accurately reflects and indicates this condition. If I report what I learned in this fashion in these pages, it is because even this small inquiry turned up what seemed to me to be matters of great and fresh interest, not only in the context of my broader concern with group identity and political change, but for their own sake. Obviously I can speak with some measure of certainty only about those individuals with whom I explored these matters most directly, but I hope it is no less obvious that I could hardly learn about them without at the same time learning something about the environment which they share with others, and without arriving at some broader view of their situation as

a group. When I do venture larger statements, however, let it be clear that they are based not on any
projection of numbers or percentages from any tabu-
lated replies to some set questions, but on my own
perceptions, judgments, and interpretations of what I
learned during this inquiry and those that have preceded it. My concern has been to do this with rigor,
care, and respect for the integrity of my informants
and their answers to my questions.

There remains something to be said about the question of bias, which I must deal with here in terms both
cautionary and personal. I do not bear the scientistic
scholar's burden of having to lay claim to a dubious
objectivity. Where such objectivity can be attained, its
limits are severe. In most sciences nowadays, it is
recognized that every observation includes the observer
as well as the observed. If this be largely true for the
natural sciences, it is wholly true for the so-called social
sciences. It has always seemed quite plain to me that
virtually all inquiry into the affairs of man is, like all
art, in some way autobiographical. Every inquirer who
concerns himself with something important in human
experience is trying to capture some elusive truth
about himself and wants at least to leave some mark to
show others where the pursuit led him and how far he
got. For my own part, I have been concerned as a
student of politics with human efforts to create a more

humane society and I do not doubt that what I have written about it could be read as the story of my own life, or at least of the hopes and glooms and styles of perceiving, thinking, and feeling that have governed my own discovery of these matters. If this has been the case where I have been concerned with Chinese and Japanese and Indians and Negro Americans and others, it clearly must be more so when I come to deal with Jews and particularly with American Jews. Given the present state of great confusion over the nature of the Jewish group identity, whether in America or in Israel, I can present myself as being as right or as wrong on the subject as the next Jew, especially any next American Jew. I feel no need to assert, as some Negroes do, that one has to be one in order to know what it's like, but there is no question that it does help. It also complicates the inquiry. Every man has to face the formidable question: "Who and what am I?" In trying to learn how Chinese, Japanese, Filipinos, Africans, and all sorts of other people are asking and answering that question, I am trying to help myself frame an answer to my own. Since every man shares his individual identity in some inescapable measure with the group of which he is inescapably part, then for me the question "Who and what am I?" must almost at once be joined to the further questions: "Who and what is an American?" And: "Who and what is a Jew?"

I am reminded here of an exchange that took place about nine years ago when a group of Negro intellectuals formed the American Society for African Culture and restricted their membership to "persons of African descent." When I asked if I might attend the organizing meeting of this group and was refused on these grounds, I reminded John A. Davis, the chairman, that the Children of Israel had spent quite some time in Egypt and who was he to say that I did not have some degree of African descent; more, possibly, even than *he* had? I was admitted, though only as an observer. It happened that on that Sunday the *Times* carried a paragraph about the findings of a demographer at Ohio State who calculated that there had to be at least 28,000,000 Americans with some African antecedents although the census showed only about 20,000,000 described as Negroes. I sent the clipping up to the chairman and in some amusement he read it to the meeting, remarking that they were obviously going to have some difficulty defining who was and who was not of "African descent." At this point a well-known Negro sociologist, never one to allow racial feelings to be confused by scholarly objectivity, jumped up and exclaimed: "Come now, when we say African descent, *we* know whom we mean!" And everybody laughed. After all, they *did* know. In much the same way, I suppose, as the cloudy, confused, but crucial debate goes on in Israel over the central question: "Who and what is a Jew?"— all the debating Jews, judges and scholars and lawyers and rabbis and kibbutzniks and bureaucrats and just plain Jews must from time to time have the same weary feeling. *They* know, they think, or at least they thought they knew until in Israel they ran not only into all those North Africans and other non-European non-white "Oriental" Jews, but also into all the new problems of definition created for them when they became a majority group and holders of a power all their own and a nationality all their own in their own country.

My encounters in Israel were with American Jews who wanted, or thought they wanted, to give primary place to their identity as Jews. I met them as an American Jew who gives primary place to his identity as an American. This difference was no doubt reflected in some way in my interviews, in the intangible elements present in each encounter, in the questions I asked and the answers I was given. Since it was precisely the ambivalence and conflict over the relationship between these two identities that became the main content of these explorations, the presence of this difference has to be noted and stressed. Just how far it imposed itself on the standards of inquiry also present—rigor, discipline, fidelity—each reader, duly warned to vigilance, will have to judge for himself.

2. Numbers

The story of American Jews in Israel is one of many versions and varieties, and these begin when you try to find out just how many of them there are. The answer you get most commonly when you ask is "About 10,000." You also hear 12,000, 15,000, even 20,000. At the American Embassy at the time of my visit, officials seemed to think that there were only "about 6,000." The most recent statement I have been able to obtain* said there were "over 20,000 Americans and Canadians in Israel," of whom 6,900 were American- or Canadian-born. If the Canadians are to be counted at their usual 10 percent of these totals, these figures have to be read as 18,000 Americans, including 6,200 American-born. The choices to be made among these widely ranging totals appeared to depend on how one counted Americans. When I pressed several of the best-informed individuals I met in Israel to make their best and most

* From David Breslau, President of the Association of Americans and Canadians in Israel, in a letter to the author, November 10, 1966.

hardheaded guesses and exclusions, what emerged was an estimate of a core of about 7,000 to 7,500 Americans who are trying to re-establish themselves as dwellers in Israel. Wherever the greatest accuracy might lie, these figures do at least indicate the range and do suggest the magnitudes. Counted at 10,000, American Jews are half of one percent of Israel's two million Jews and less than two-tenths of a percent of America's five and a half million. They are, then, a tiny group, but just how tiny is hard to say without grasping for some elusive facts.

What, for example, quizzically asked one of my informants on this matter, do you do about the children? Do you count them? Many of the American immigrants of recent years were young people, and many young couples among them started their families in Israel. Many (nobody could even guess how many) Americans have married Israelis of other origins— "mixed marriages" according to the joke idiom in this group—and have their children coming along. Technically, the children of American citizens have until they reach age eighteen to choose to be or not to be American citizens themselves, but with only the rarest exceptions, youngsters of these families reaching this age go into the Israeli armed services as the local law requires and thereby automatically choose to become citizens of Israel. Some American families try to keep American influences alive in their homes and to raise these children bilingually in Hebrew and in English.

But this is a difficult thing to do even for the younger immigrants. As their own immigrant grandparents or parents in America had learned, the pull of the outside environment is irresistibly stronger than that of the home and children generally have an overpowering need not to be "different." Among the children of older American immigrants in Israel, awareness of America is often even more dim and knowledge of English rudimentary or halting. I had one conversation with some "American" teen-agers in which one of their fathers had to act as interpreter. They evidently knew some English, but were unwilling to use it. Like most children of immigrants, they wanted to melt into the surrounding majority of their locally born peers. In Israel they come up in an environment peculiarly marked by a certain ambivalence not only about Americans and American Jews but sometimes even about the English language. This often leaves their American parents—whose own parents had gone through similar experiences in the American environment only a generation before—in a position poignant or pathetic and always painfully ironic.

At the other end of the age scale, there are older folks included in some of the larger totals of "Americans" whose connection to America is a good deal more tenuous than that of these youngsters. These are people who came from America to Palestine in the earlier immigrations, beginning with a tiny trickle before the First World War and growing to a total of somewhere between 3,000 and 5,000 by the time of the

Second World War. In the later years of this period of migrations, some of the migrants were younger people who had been born in America (664 out of 2,500 between 1935 and 1942 according to one account), but they remained a small minority. The great majority were individuals who had migrated first from Eastern Europe to America and then, after some years, re-emigrated to Palestine. A few of these earlier Zionist settlers achieved prominence in Israel—Russian-born Golda Meir, who served as the Israeli Foreign Minister, lived some years of her youth in Milwaukee before coming to Palestine in the early 1920s—but it is doubtful if any of them would even now think of themselves as Americans. They and their children have largely been absorbed into the socially and politically dominant group of Eastern European old-timers in Israel of which they were really part and they are far removed in any of their present identifications from the Americans who have come to Israel in more recent years. For some purposes of record-keeping or record-claiming, one attempt was made to make the number of older American pioneers more inclusive by establishing quite arbitrarily that five years' residence in the United States was enough to count a person as "American" in arriving at the grand totals over time. This criterion was established by some leaders of the Association of Americans and Canadians in Israel,* but only a small number, it seems, could be added to the roster

* P. E. Lapide, *A Century of U.S. Aliya*, Association of Americans and Canadians in Israel, Jerusalem, 1961, pp. 27–28, 138.

by this means. There is a relatively substantial number of European-born Americans over sixty-five (estimated at 1,500 in 1963) who have come to Israel since the founding of the state who certainly belong in any roster of Americans in Israel, but there are greater numbers of other European-born migrants from America who can be included in the American total only by the most generous stretching of their American connection, and it apparently takes the utmost of this kind of generosity to arrive at the maximum figure of 20,000.

Such a figure would also no doubt include another somewhat exotic group of "American" Jews in Israel whose inclusion in these statistics is at least an arguable matter. These are members of a number of ultra-orthodox sects who hold American passports either because they were naturalized while living in America or because they were born there. At the time of my visit they were said to number about 1,000, living in their own separate small communities in Israel; later figures are put higher. Most of the elders among them made their way to refuge in America from Hitler-threatened Eastern Europe. Their American-born children were raised, with but rare exceptions, entirely within the closed culture of their sects. Although the more extreme among them do not accept the statehood of Israel (because it did not come about through the appearance of the Messiah), many have settled there, joining older fellow communities or forming new ones of their own. They are said to be even more zealous about retaining their American citizenship than other Americans in Israel. They stand distinctly apart from the recognizable American constituency and even more apart from the Israeli mass. Since I did not learn myself at first hand how they locate themselves in this spectrum of groups, they certainly are a group apart from those considered and described in this report.

According to the record published by the Association, the total of immigrants to Palestine from America from 1860 to 1948 was about 7,000, out of a grand total of all immigrants to Palestine in this time of about 500,000. The total of American immigrants who came and stayed between 1948 and mid-1960 is given in this account as a net figure of 7,595. One says "net" because it is estimated for every one who came and stayed, there were five or more who came and, after a time, left. In 1959 a former president of the Association estimated that 6,000 Americans had remained out of a total of 35,000 who had come. Of 1,700 Americans who came in 1948 to help fight to win and hold the state, about one-fourth, one is told, either remained or returned later to settle in the country they had helped to create. Other estimates or guesses I heard put the ratio somewhat more favorably for more recent years, between 1,500 and 2,000 Americans arriving as prospective settlers each year and about 1,000 leaving. A compilation of figures published in December, 1964, raised the estimated net number of American immigrants for the period since 1948 to 10,400.* This would be the American total out of the grand total of one and a half million Jews who came to the new state from many other places during this same period of time. By its own report in mid-1964, the Association of Americans and Canadians in Israel had 4,000 families registered with it (approximately 10 percent of them Canadian). Its bulletin was being published in an edition of 8,000 of which 2,500 were going to readers abroad.** At the end of 1966, the president of the association reported*** that "we now have 7,500 cards in our office," including 2,000 listing single individuals and 5,500 couples. He said there was hope that a census could be taken, in a year or so, that would finally pin down some of these elusive facts and figures. Subject to correction by such a census, here is how several of the most knowledgeable of my informants sorted out the numbers and locations of American Jewish settlers in Israel at that time. They were counting only adults and combined all the best available estimates and guesses to arrive at the following:

—About 2,000 individuals engaged in agriculture. According to a report made to the Association in March, 1963, a count had been made of 789 Americans on 94 kibbutzim, 239 Americans on 34 moshavim, or cooperatives, and 200 in private agriculture, operating

* *A Century of U.S. Aliya,* p. 129; P. E. Lapide, "American Aliya: Past Facts and Future Hopes," *Jewish Frontier,* December, 1964, p. 14.
** *Bulletin* of the AACI, May, 1964, p. 13.
*** In a letter to the author dated December 26, 1966.

family farms, orange groves, in one case raising beef cattle and in others, more recently, flowers. It was not clear how this total of 1,228 dealt with families and children, or how far the actual identification as American was established. A majority of those on the land are of the older pre-1948 and immediately post-1948 immigrant generation, their ranks increased only by rather small numbers added in more recent years. These farming Americans will be found, however, in all parts of this tiny country, along the fertile coastal plain, in the bare hills of the north where their settlements are often within sight (and shooting range) of the closed borders of Syria or Jordan, on scattered patches of green drilled and dug out of the Negev in the south where the desert runs up against the Gaza strip and the enemy land of Egypt in the southwest and skirts close to other Arab hostility where it comes to its narrow end at Elath in the deep south on the Gulf of Aqaba.

—About 1,500, some of them ex-kibbutzniks, almost all of them post-1948 immigrants, working in private professional or semiprofessional capacities as teachers, scientists, engineers, doctors, nurses, technicians of various kinds, often on the staffs of various institutions in the educational, health, welfare, or related fields, or in some of the major scientific, industrial, or construction enterprises of the government. They are to be found living in Israel's three main cities, Jerusalem, Tel Aviv, and Haifa, and a few in some of the "new towns" springing up to meet the needs of this bulging little nation. For most of them, however, the prized place to live is in Jerusalem where, even in its newer parts atop its Judaean hills separated by barbed wire and barriers from the older sections of the city that are now located in the hostile state of Jordan, they still can feel that they are breathing the air of distant ages long gone. The magic of the city's name itself, helped a bit by restraints on building styles and materials imposed by the government, have managed somehow to keep it a place where it remains possible to feel a connection to the remote past, a link to the time and the people of the Bible.

—About 300 American immigrants who have gone into private business. They are mostly concentrated in Tel Aviv. Most of them are in small (estimated typical capital, $50,000) retail or wholesaling enterprises or small factories in metal fabrication, plastics, motors, repair shops, and the like. American enterprise has introduced the supermarket to Jerusalem and Tel Aviv. Sizable amounts of American capital, but very few American individuals, are to be found in the small number of larger industrial and construction firms now operating in the country. In the small business community, Americans are a tiny minority and a rather embattled one. They are scarcely visible in the crowded city of Tel Aviv, a metropolis of some 400,000 which Jewish immigrants began to develop about forty years ago. Here you can find exemplars of all the stereotypes classically attached to Eastern European

Diaspora Jews, including what Jerusalem residents dis-
dainfully call "that element" in commerce, and also a
stunning new concert hall where a symphony orchestra
plays to packed audiences, and where a new university
has recently risen to challenge the long-standing
monopoly of Jerusalem's Hebrew University in the
realm of higher education.

—Another small cluster of about 300 Americans in
government jobs. They are all civil servants at the
middle or upper middle levels of Israel's flourishing
bureaucracy. There are no Americans in posts of political power—unless you count Golda Meir as an
"American"—and none at the top in any field, unless
again one counts as "American" someone like Simon
Agranat, now President—i.e., Chief Justice—of the
Supreme Court, who is probably the most highly
placed "American" in the country. His father first
settled in Palestine in 1922, he came himself in 1930,
became a judge under the British mandate long before
the state came into being. The other most prominent
semi-American is an ex-Canadian, Dov Joseph, who
served as Minister of Justice, who came to Palestine in
the 1920s from Eastern Europe via Canada. Of the
younger and more identifiably American immigrants,
one I met was a chief scientific adviser, and several
were working as relatively obscure but sometimes influential aides and secretaries in key ministries. An
American specialist conducted Israel's first census and
when I met him he was head of its manpower com-

mission. Another was running a government aircraft
assembly plant. The senior civil servant in the Ministry of the Interior at the time of my visit was an
American and so was one of the top officers of the
police establishment. A few had reached similar places
in the Ministry of Defense and in the armed services.

—An estimated 2,000 American women listed as
"non-working wives" of these assorted urban settlers, a
description that hardly fits the lives they lead in making and keeping their homes and raising their children
in the conditions available to them. There are also
women among the professionals and other specialists in
the urban groups and also, of course, among those on
the kibbutzim or other rural establishments.

—The special group, finally, of about 1,500 Americans who are called "senior residents." These are men
and women over sixty-five years of age who have come
to Israel from America to live out their retirement
with the help of their Social Security checks. They are
almost all immigrants who first came to America from
Eastern Europe a lifetime ago and have chosen to come
at the end to the land of the Zionist dream. Some of
them live in special homes and hostels supported by
various organizations to which they belong back home
in America, others in their own independent, costlier,
but lonely little apartments—some in softer, older
Haifa up the coast, a few scattered around living near
children settled on the land, but most of them in the
big city of Tel Aviv where it is easiest for them to come

together or to find friends of their own age and backgrounds.

Such, then, are the Americans settled in Israel, 7,600 of them listed this way, and as many others, young and old, as one wants to add to arrive at the alternative totals of 10,000, 12,000, 15,000, or 20,000. They are not to be confused with tourists who come in swarms (70,000 in 1964, 80,000 in 1965) or with Americans who come as students (about 500 in 1965) for a year or so, although some "tourists" do come to look and stay for long periods, and some become "commuters" who move back and forth at intervals of months or years. We are dealing here with those American Jews who either are, or are trying to become, permanent dwellers in Israel, "olim" or settlers, or at least people who are trying to think of themselves in this way. Together with the 7,000 Jews from England, the 4,500 from South Africa, and the much smaller numbers who come from Canada and Australia, they are the settlers in Israel who are generally called, of all things, "the Anglo-Saxons."

3. Name To Go By: The "Anglo-Saxons"

The first time I heard the term "Anglo-Saxon" applied to American Jews in Israel was in a conversation with a visiting Israeli professor in Cambridge a few years ago. He was surprised at my surprise and a full half-minute slow in joining my laugh at the sardonic humor of it. For him, the irony had long since been rubbed off the term by familiar use, and this seemed to be generally the case among Israelis I met in Israel. But I found many of the "Anglo-Saxons" themselves uncomfortably self-conscious about the term, avoiding it and trying, not very successfully, to discourage its use by others. A prime example was the case of the "Anglo-Saxon Shikun," a new block of 62 comfortable apartments still being completed in Jerusalem when I was there, a long, low two-story structure in the city's characteristic stone lying flat along the rocky slopes just below the imposing buildings of Hebrew University.

This shikun, or housing project, was put up by and for a group of well-established residents, almost all Americans, each one paying sums of up to £50,000 (about $17,000) to purchase his apartment, with some financial and other assistance arranged by the project's sponsors, the Association of Americans and Canadians in Israel. From the outset, the place had automatically been named the "Anglo-Saxon Shikun." When its resident owners got together, they tried to give it a different name, some wits suggesting a name that included both the idea of being on the heights and enjoying a higher standard of living. This would not have been exactly libelous, for these modest two-and-three-bedroom apartments are positively luxurious by present Israeli housing standards, but even under what is called "normalization" in Israel nowadays no one, least of all Americans, likes to emphasize economic inequalities. What they settled on, finally, was "Nayot," a word out of the Bible meaning "a pleasant place"; which indeed it is in housing-arched Israel.* The official name on the sign at the entering road is AMERICAN-CANADIAN HOUSING PROJECT IN JERUSALEM—NAYOT. But to taxi drivers and to everyone else, it has remained simply the "Anglo-Saxon Shikun" or, in Hebrew, "Shikun Anglo-Saxi." Said one of its occupants testily: "Nobody likes the term. I don't like it.

* For a picture of life in the "Anglo-Saxon Shikun" by one of the inhabitants see Yehuda Lev, "And he went and dwelt in Nayot," "Israel Seen From Within," *Jewish Frontier,* December, 1964.

It's an Israeli term. I'm not Anglo and I'm not Saxon. We used to fight it, but I guess we have given up on it now." A similarly named development of small but pleasant single-family homes built mainly for Americans at Herzlia, a suburb of Tel Aviv, was more successfully redubbed "the American shikun," the term "American" carrying with it in Israel its own freight of separateness and ambivalence but at least a label much more naturally and legitimately borne by American Jews than "Anglo-Saxon."

As used by many Israelis, "Anglo-Saxon" apparently carries with it not irony but more often a certain sting of malice and envy only sometimes mixed with grudging admiration. The "Anglo-Saxons" are generally seen as better-off, better-educated, more privileged people who did not personally experience the holocaust and who therefore, unlike so many European immigrants, still have families intact and living, parents, even grandparents, people who did not come to Israel because they had to but because they chose to—a fact that made them "fools" in the eyes of some Israelis, "true idealists" in the eyes of some others—and who, most of all, have somewhere to go back to if they want to leave. All of this applies to almost all of the "Anglo-Saxons" and most particularly to the Americans and it stings because it is all usually quite true. Hence the mixed feelings and the discomfort caused by the term among the "Anglo-Saxons" themselves. But I would guess at other reasons too for their discomfort, more complex and obscure. There are faint but unmistakable marks of old snobbisms about Anglo-Saxon superiority rubbed into parts of this picture. There are also some deeper feelings and associations. To at least some of these displaced Americans and Britons in Israel, I suspect, the values of Anglo-Saxon culture and society are much more real than assumed, their own yearning for identification with it strong, their feelings about it tender and sore, because though they had accepted it, they felt it had failed to accept them; and this may be why, in no small measure, some of them left home. For such individuals to acquire finally in Israel an identity as "Anglo-Saxons"—or even simply to be labeled as such—is a paradox whose sardonic humor they could not possibly always appreciate.

Actually, as far as I could discover, the use of the term began not in irony, envy or malice, but as a matter of bureaucratic convenience which involved a far broader and far more ironic use of national labels for the various segments of the great masses of immigrants who crowded into Israel during the last thirty years. The Jewish Agency, an extra-governmental body which had responsibility for handling this massive immigration, was organized into sets of "national" sections, much like the geographic "desks" in a typical foreign office. Like these "desks," each Jewish Agency section bore the name of its particular country—the Polish, the Lithuanian, the Rumanian, the Czech, and so on. For all the many purposes of immigration and absorption, these national sections handled their people as groups and referred to them in the handiest way, i.e., by their national labels. For many, if not for most of them, this was an unaccustomed identification; indeed, it had marked in the most explicit way their status in their home countries that they were "Jews," not "Poles" or "Rumanians" and most emphatically not "Algerians," "Moroccans" or "Egyptians." It was only when they came to Palestine, later Israel, to embrace a new nationality of their own in the Jewish homeland that they finally acquired the nationality labels they had largely been denied in the lands that had been their homes for so long. There was at least one exception to this practice; it would have been a bit too much, even in this land of paradoxes, for the Jews who came in masses from Hitler's Germany in the 1930s to have become known as "the Germans." Their organization was once formally called Hitachdut Olei Germania but Germans generally acquired the nickname "Yeckes" which was attached to the firstcomers and has stuck ever since. "Yeckes" literally means "jackets" and had to do with the tie-and-jacket neatness of the middle-class Germans who came to Palestine and presented such an always tidy, always trim, very urban bourgeois contrast to the non-jacket-wearing, open-shirt-collared, purposively nonbourgeois Eastern European pioneers they joined there. In time, the name "Yeckes" took on all the qualities of the standard German stereotype: neat, precise, formal, rigid, effi-

cient, and, on the whole, rather unimaginatively intelligent.* Among the others, I found Latvian and
Esthonian Jews being called "the Balts" (what pre-
sumption that would have been in old Riga!) —one
kibbutz I visited that was made up of groups of Americans and Latvians and a few English families was
known as the "Anglo-Balt kibbutz." More generally I
was told, Jews from the Baltic countries are known as
"the Litvaks," a term of common usage in other immigrant settings.

In the case of the various "Anglo-Saxon" Jews the
use of national labels had different ironic weights suggesting the different specific gravities of separateness of
Jews in the English-speaking countries. I asked the
young grandmotherly secretary of the British Settlers
Association how English Jews felt about being called
"Anglo-Saxon." She laughed an arch little laugh. "It's
become quite a joke," she said. "In all our memos we
use 'British settlers' and avoid 'Anglo-Saxons.' It is
something we are trying to get away from." When I
asked her how the English and the Americans got on
together she indicated that some of her best friends
were Americans, and added that, what was more, her
daughter had actually married one. The Jews from
England and other ex-dominions are usually of much
the same background as the majority of American

* Another explanation of "Yeckes" offered by one informant made it
an acronym of the Hebrew words *Yehudi Keshi Havanah,* meaning "Jews
with difficulty in understanding"—i.e., "rigid."

Jews, products of the migrations from Eastern Europe that began in the 1880s and continued down to about 1920, with accretions in the 1930s from Germany and other Hitler-threatened countries in Central and Eastern Europe. A few Jews have reached high places in English society but Jews generally have occupied a quite distinctly separate place of their own. They became "British" but this did not make them "Englishmen" (and certainly not Scots or Welsh) or, for that matter, "Australians" or "Canadians," and in South Africa were set even more distinctively apart as one section of the English-speaking community. In all these cases they did share a common identity with all the others under the much wider, looser rubric of British subjectdom, a realm that used to include all sorts of people from Greenwich both ways to the international date line. This "British" identity had *pluribus* to spare, but its only *unum* (aside, perhaps, from an Oxbridge degree) was the Crown.

By contrast, the "American" identity is differently made, proposing an all-embracing inclusiveness that would make "Americans" out of all the many different kinds and groups of people who have come to make up the American nation. The ideal holds any imposed separateness to be a violation of the national credo, any self-chosen separateness a right of any group or person subject only to the common rights of all. For a long time, as everybody knows, this was more preachment than practice, especially for non-whites, non-Anglo-

Saxons, non-Protestants, and non-North-Europeans. But for quite a while now, it has been theory-painfully-becoming-fact, and this, both as goal and as partial reality, has more than anything else created the uniqueness of the "American" identity. This is what marks off American Jews from their many fellow Jews of common European origin only two or three generations back, fixed a special relationship between American Jewry and Israel, and remains stamped hard even on this small number of American Jews who felt driven by some lack in their lives as "Americans" to migrate to Israel to try to give priority to living as "Jews." In Israel it is what marks off the "Americans," even from their fellow "Anglo-Saxons." A very special mix of things is indicated, therefore, when some of these Americans, reaching for their share of the common Israeli lot, say ruefully in their turn: "In America we were 'Jews.' In Israel we become 'Americans.' "

These differences are partly reflected in the way the various "Anglo-Saxons" have sorted themselves out in different national combinations. Among the distinctive organizations formed by the various national groups, we find the Americans and Canadians together in the Association of Americans and Canadians in Israel, the Australians and New Zealanders joined with the British in the British Settlers Association, and the South Africans by themselves in an Israel section of the South African Zionist Federation. It was not until 1964 that a common center was established in Tel Aviv for the use of members of all these groups, and although the Jewish agency has accommodatingly changed the name of its section from "Anglo-Saxon" to "Western Aliya" (i.e., Section for Western Immigration), each group maintains its separate existence, preserving its special characteristics, habits, attitudes, and antipathies, sharing only in the vague and embarrassing luster and special status that comes from being "Anglo-Saxons" in Israel.

The three "Anglo-Saxon" organizations are only three of dozens of such national groupings, *landsmannschaft* organizations, in which people of common origins come together, partly to deal as a group with the formidable Israeli bureaucracy, partly to enable older-timers to help bewildered newcomers, and also to provide a place where each of these many species can flock together, be with their "own" kind, hear their "own" language spoken freely again, and share all the tangible and intangible samenesses of their common backgrounds. The newer the immigrant, the greater his need for these supporting bonds, but even among the older ones, as their Hebrew-speaking children pull away from them to give their own new shape to what is called "the Jewish life" in Israel, there is often, it seems, a continuing need to belong to nationality groups although as nationals of these many countries, they were so often not allowed to "belong" at all. Jews have come to Israel, it is commonly said in the old phrase, from "70 countries," meaning from all over the

world, and I was told that there were at one time as
many as 45 *landsmannschaft* organizations in existence.
By attrition, splits, and mergers, this had come down to
about 30, although no one seemed sure of this number
either. Besides the three "Anglo-Saxon" groups already
named, the European groups included the Bulgarian,
Belgian, Bessarabian, Bukovinian (the last two being
split-offs from the Rumanian which still maintains
itself separately) , Czech, Dutch, Hungarian, Latvian
and Esthonian, Lithuanian, Polish, Scandinavian, and
Yugoslav. There were once separate German and Aus-
trian groups, but these have been merged into a single
"Central European" association. Some special groups
have been formed out of shared experiences more
salient than former nationalities, e.g., the Association
of Survivors of Belsen and Association of Survivors of
Concentration Camps of Greek Origin. There is the
currently very active Association of Latin American
Settlers with a constituency, I was told, of somewhere
between 12,000 and 15,000, the largest number from
Argentina, with more arriving each month. Among the
Asian and African Jews, there are associations of
settlers from Afghanistan, India, and Iraq (the Iraqis
use the Hebrew name *Bavel,* which means Babylonia,
although for all other official purposes in Israel, Iraq is
Iraq) . There is also a Turkish association, an Egyptian,
a Libyan, an Algerian, and a Moroccan, with the latter
trying to be somewhat more inclusive by calling itself
the "North African" group—a term allowing its mem-

bers also to escape the strongly negative burden carried by the name "Moroccan." The appearance in Israel of a great mass of non-European Jews—now more than half the population—has created the core problem of the new society being created there and this is reflected in some other terminological twists. It has given new content to the traditional division between Ashkenazi and Sephardi Jews but has also made "Western" Jews out of the traditional "East European" Jews and "Eastern" or "Oriental" Jews out of the Sephardi, even if they come from as far west, geographically, as Morocco (from the Maghreb—the Arabic term for North Africa that actually means "the West"). Other terms for these non-European Jews, all pejorative, include "Franks," for French-speaking North Africans, and "Kurdi" (i.e., from Kurdistan) and "cushi" or "schwartze," the Hebrew and Yiddish vernacular terms for black, because most of the so-called "Oriental" Jews are dark in color. There is also in Israel, I was somewhat startled to find, an Association of Settlers from China, but its members are not any of the famous Chinese Jews from Honan, but European Jews who fled to China at various times in the last thirty or forty years—the two main waves fleeing the Bolsheviks in Russia after 1917 and the Nazis in Germany after 1933—and who now in Israel seemingly find more to share out of their common China experience than out of their remoter European identifications. They are not, however, called "the Chinese" but the "Jews from China" or "immigrants from China."

In Hebrew the name of these various national or *landsmannschaft* groups follows a uniform pattern. Each is known as Hitachdut (Association) of Olei (Immigrants from) such and such a country. The name of the American-Canadian group in Hebrew is just like all the others: Hitachdut Olei America Canada. In English, however, it is called the *Association of Americans and Canadians in Israel.* In this difference between the name in Hebrew and the name in English— i.e., the elimination of the word *olei*—lies the heart of the story of these American Jews in Israel; tiny as it is, this detail lights up the dilemma in which they have placed themselves and the ambivalence in which all but a few of them painfully live.

The word *olei* is a plural form of *oleh,* which is usually translated as "immigrant" though it actually means "one who ascends," meaning that someone who comes to Israel is rising to a higher destiny, to a higher realm of the spirit, and is not to be confused with a mere immigrant who, like the millions of immigrants who went to the United States a few generations ago, were seeking a better material life. The *olim* who come to Israel are, in Zionist terminology, to be seen as seekers after social and spiritual integration as Jews in the land of the Bible, the home of Jewish history. Hence the *aliya* or "ascent." Backsliding olim who re-emigrate from Israel to go elsewhere to the United

States if they possibly can are called *yordim,* or "people descending."* In this idealized vocabulary, to be an oleh is to be reaching for something not far from the equivalent of what Christians call "grace" and to be a *yored* (singular of yordim) is to come fairly close to falling back down into a state of sin, if not into hell itself.

Now it is this question of being an oleh, or less poetically, simply an immigrant, that sharply and uncomfortably divides most American Jews in Israel from the greater mass of Israelis among whom they come to live. Almost all the million and a half Jews who have crowded into Israel since 1948 came not as idealistic pioneers but as refugees fleeing from the actuality of persecution or the fear of it. They were, in the Zionist vernacular, more "pushed" than "pulled." They came in under the unique Law of Return whereby all Jews were automatically and instantly accepted as Israeli citizens upon arrival in the state. Hence they came as olim, rising to whatever higher level Israel could raise them as Jews. By contrast, all but a small handful of

* Official Israeli records show that 110,000 *yordim* left Israel between 1948 and 1963, including just under 21,000 persons born in Israel, to an idealistic Zionist the most mortifying kind of *yordim* of all. Cf. *Statistical Abstract of Israel,* Central Bureau of Statistics, Jerusalem, No. 17, 1966, p. 105. An unknown number of these *yordim* are Jews who came to Israel only to acquire Israeli passports and promptly left to settle elsewhere. Under the Law of Return this procedure could be completed in one or two weeks. To curb this abuse of the Israeli nationality, the Knesset amended the Law in August 1966 requiring a year's residence before citizenship may be granted and setting up new requirements for passport renewals for Israeli citizens living abroad. Cf. *New York Times,* August 4, 1966.

the Americans who came in this way did come as "idealists," or as idealizers of the promise of Zion, or, at the very least, came of their own choice. Whatever it was they were fleeing, it was not persecution or danger in their homeland. They were truly much more "pulled" than "pushed." But it has been the rare arriving American in these years who has come in under the Law of Return as an oleh. Instead Americans take the choice that Israeli law gives them and "opt out" of Israeli citizenship. They come in—virtually without exception nowadays—as "temporary residents" and after holding on to this status as long as possible in due course become "permanent residents," remaining American citizens throughout. This becomes, as we have already suggested and shall show further in some detail, the central paradox of their experience of migration. This is why, although the Hebrew name of the Association identifies its members as "olei" or "immigrants" there is a certain sensitivity to the use of this term in English and all the alternatives remain uncomfortably ambiguous. "We prefer to use the term 'settler,' " one of their leading spokesmen told me. On the other hand, when an attempt was made in 1961 to change the group's name to "American and Canadian Settlers Association," an embarrassed argument rose that this would seem to exclude all those who retained status not as "settlers" but as "residents" and the matter was left unresolved, a condition in which it has remained ever since.

Sometimes, but by no means always, a change of individual name is an indicator of the choice a person has made. Some of the earlier enthusiasts who came as *halutzim,* or pioneers, to win and work the Holy Land shed not only their American citizenship but also the names they had acquired in the Diaspora and adopted Hebrew names instead. "This kind of thing was happening more widely in the bravo days when people were adopting new identities in the formal as well as in the informal sense," explained one of those who had come in that time but had himself, for reasons he found it difficult to cite, kept the name he came with. "It is less common now," he went on, "for Americans who are not becoming citizens would find it most embarrassing. The government usually likes people who represent it abroad for any purpose to have Hebrew names, and in one or two cases this has created sticky situations for some of the people concerned." One meets Americans with Hebrew names more often on the kibbutzim than in the cities. Names are not indicative of citizenship status, however, since some citizens have retained their old name while some noncitizens have assumed Hebrew names for professional or other reasons connected with their jobs.

Some of the oddly mixed feelings that get stirred up in this matter of names are suggested by a story told about one of the most vigorously and happily integrated Americans I met in Israel, a successful young businessman named Raphael ben Yosef, who was

Raphael Finkel when he came over from Baltimore in 1948, fresh out of the United States Marines, to fight for Israel. After he had settled down, become an Israeli citizen, and adopted his new name, his father came over to visit him and indicated some unhappiness over the name change. "Why did he have to do it?" he testily asked one of his son's friends. "Wasn't Finkel good enough for him?" The friend remonstrated. "But, Mr. Finkel, he's now ben Yosef—son of Yosef—and that's *you!* That does you even greater honor, doesn't it?" Indeed, by the new Israeli custom, the newly adopted Hebrew name does not shift each generation to so-and-so the son of so-and-so but remains a permanent surname, any son of Raphael ben Yosef's remaining "ben Yosef" rather than becoming "ben Raphael." The elderly Mr. Finkel from Baltimore was not pleased or appeased. "No," he said stubbornly. "The name is Finkel. It was good enough for me and should be good enough for him!"

4. Why They Came

Most American Jews in Israel are wrestling with a great tangle of problems of everyday living, which are hard, and a greater array of problems of life, which are harder. They are struggling with "insiderness" and "outsiderness," with being "American," being "Jewish" and being "Israeli," with discovering what culture they are part of or want to be part of, deciding what kind of life they want and where and how they want to live it, what nationality to claim, what passport to carry —a formidable series of dilemmas, demands, and unanswered riddles. In the end somehow, by act or by default, each individual must decide where he *belongs*. Much of all this comes out of the special and unique circumstances into which these Americans come, but much of what happens to them is wrapped up in the reasons why they came to Israel in the first place.

These reasons are many and mixed, idealistic and ideological, peculiar and personal, varying greatly by background and by the time of coming, and by a host of individual uniquenesses. One individual, indeed, suggested that since their numbers were so small, it was probably the most personal and idiosyncratic reasons that came closest to explaining anyone's behavior. These were not often easily identified and some of those I met seemed weary of trying to figure it all out. "I've stopped asking people why they came," dryly said one American I met during my first few days in the country. "They might tell me." It was his way of turning my question away from himself, and I was reminded of his self-protective device a few days later when I put the same question to a mild man in his middle forties who was working as a bookkeeper on a kibbutz. His rather emphatic and highly verbal wife had just left their room. "I guess I married into it," he said with a tired smile.

Many of these reasons remained elusive, and the feelings underlying them often even more so, and in some cases this might very well have been because they had to do not with being an American or a Jew but with being one's own peculiar and troubled self with problems that one was trying to solve by running off from one place to another. Many people mentioned this as a factor, but almost always, of course, in talking about somebody else. "Anybody who can't make it at home is not going to make it here either," said one long-established settler. A European psychiatrist in Jerusalem told me that he had found his American patients—he acknowledged that he had only two or three—to be "alienated people to begin with, uprooted from themselves, without a good identity of their own, not feeling good about belonging in their surroundings at home and therefore failing to feel good about their surroundings here." I have no doubt that there are some American Jews in Israel who do not yet know that one cannot alter the drama of one's life by simply changing the scene. I met one restless man who had been unable to make up his mind about his life for years and now had brought his unwilling wife to Israel to see if he could find what he wanted there. Another was a middle-aged spinster left adrift when her mother died and when her best Gentile friends turned out to be polite anti-Semites. I was told that there had been eleven cases the previous year of mentally ill people who had been shipped off to Israel by relatives in America and who had been shipped right back to America by health officials in Israel.

It is possible to classify alarming percentages of almost any group of people as mentally or emotionally disturbed and I have no way of knowing or guessing about such percentages among American Jews in Israel. On the other hand, the larger and plainer fact remains that Jews generally, whether in Israel or in America or elsewhere, suffer from rootlessness not because they are alienated personalities in the first place but because they are Jews. They all belong to a group of people for whom alienation, separation, exclusion, rejection, and marginality have been the chronic conditions of life for so long that they have shaped many of the defensively ingrown features of their group life and even some elements of a common personality shared in some degree by all. These are precisely some of the features of the Jewish group identity that come up now for drastic and challenging revision. The great mass of American Jews is in the process of shedding the condition of rootlessness by becoming integrated in the American society. This is producing cries of alarm over the threatened disappearance of the group through assimilation. It is also requiring American Jews to define their Jewishness by something other than their outsiderness. How this great mass of Jews is getting on with this process in Gentile America is a large subject filling many people's minds and a great deal of public print. What we are concerned with here, however, is the tiny handful of American Jews who have chosen to try to overcome this common condition by migrating to Israel. They are American Jews who argue in effect that Jews will never really be able to "belong" success-fully in Gentile America or that they will "belong" much more successfully as Jews in the Jewish State of Israel. Whole backgrounds, styles of life, and ways of coping with existence in Israel are folded into the reasons these American Jews give for their act of migration. These reasons often overlap or shade into one another, but they do sort out different kinds, roughly mark off some special groups, and explain in some part the varying levels of their commitment and the varying degrees of their success in trying to "belong" in Israel.

Perhaps the most clearly marked among these migrants are those who came out of strongly Zionist-oriented immigrant families in America, or out of Zionist youth groups there, or, more usually, out of both, and as a result found themselves headed away from America and toward the Land of Israel from a very early age. There is no way of saying precisely just how many of the American Jews now in Israel came out of this background. The chances are that they would include almost all who are engaged in agriculture, and especially those who are presently on the kibbutzim as collective farmers. It was a cardinal tenet of Zionist ideology that Jews should not only return to the Land of Israel, but that they should literally return to the land as pioneering tillers, ceasing to be urban captives of the Exile, condemned to be merchants and traders and manipulators of money. From the great stream of immigrants that began to flow west from Eastern Europe in the 1880s, small rivulets were deflected southward by the first dreamers of the Zionist dream who went to Palestine as pioneers. The greater masses who went to America were caught up there by another dream, the American dream, and it was out of its stuff that their lives and the lives of their children and grandchildren were largely woven. They became today's five and a half million American Jews, most of whom dutifully contribute to the Zionist cause but never even remotely think of this as implying their own ultimate migration to a regained Jewish homeland. Among the Jews who came to America, however, there was a small band of the Zionist faithful who thought of themselves as having come to America only as a stopping place on their way to Palestine. A small number of these individuals did actually re-emigrate to Palestine after a few years in America—nearly 2,000 of them went to join the Jewish Legion to fight with the British army in the reconquest of Palestine in the First World War and of these about 500 became settlers.* Many more remained faithful, but only after their own fashion, living on in America while continuing to dream the Zionist dream and passing it on to their children.

Most commonly these children, like their Zionist fathers, fell or half-fell by the American wayside, displacing the promised commitment to Palestine by an actual commitment to America. But some of them remained successfully transient in the spirit of their upbringing. While the general disaffection and alienation of the 1930s was sending so many young people in search of radical solutions for their ills, some of these young sojourners were finding their outlets in Zionist youth groups which were either religious or socialist in

* *A Century of U.S. Aliya*, pp. 65–66.

orientation. These were essentially political organizations in the tradition of older Zionist groups going back to the turn of the century. In accordance with both Jewish and socialist custom, they were usually divided into several parts. Thus among the socialists there were various factions and groups of which the most important were the social democratic Zionist Labor Organization and its youth group, Habonim ("The Builders") , and the more Communist oriented or "left-wing" Hashomer Hatzair ("Young Guards") which had been founded in Poland and transplanted in 1928 to the United States. Both groups held collectivist ideas about the proper way of returning to the soil. They pursued their separate doctrinal ways in quite separate communal settlements, the famous kibbutzim, in Israel. Some religious groups—the Labor Zionists were more or less militantly nonreligious—also followed their bents in their own separate communities. They all taught "aliya" or settlement in Israel as life's highest purpose and gave special training in the United States to convert young urban Americans into land-reclaiming pioneers in Israel. Of the several thousands ("probably close to 10,000," according to one estimate) who joined these groups through the 1930s and 1940s, some much smaller number eventually did reach Palestine, or, after 1948, the new State of Israel. They went in small groups to join established kibbutzim or to join with European immigrants to found new ones. A first small group of these American

settlers founded the kibbutz Ein Hashofet in 1937.
One estimate by one of these pioneers was that of all
who had come to Israel under the auspices of these two
main groups, there were now perhaps fewer than a
thousand survivors scattered on some sixteen kibbutzim around the country, each with its own strictly
maintained doctrinal allegiance and party affiliation,
and perhaps a similar number of former members
who had left the kibbutzim but were still living and
working in Israel in other settings.

This Zionist background turned up clearly and
quickly among the answers I began to get when I asked
Americans why they had come to Israel, especially
among those who by Israeli standards could be regarded as veteran settlers.

- "My parents originally intended to come to Palestine but came to America instead in 1921," said an Ivy
League Ph.D. in his late thirties. "At eleven I joined
the Zionist youth movement in New York. I grew up
with the intention of coming to Palestine, to go on a
kibbutz, to become an ideological farmer, and in 1949
I came."

- "I came of an old Zionist family always oriented
on Israel," said a university professor in his forties.
"There was always the sense of being transient in the
United States. Then when my wife and I were married
in 1944, we never set up a home, for we expected to be
going to Palestine."

- "My parents came from Rumania to the United

States as a way station on the way to Palestine and they eventually did come here," said a newspaper editor. "When I graduated from Cornell in 1930 they were here, I came to join them, and I stayed."

• "My father came to the United States in 1913. He was a Zionist and worked as a milkman," said a teacher of physics in a kibbutz high school. "I went into the Zionist youth movement at thirteen or fourteen, and I was about seventeen in the late 1930s when I decided to come to Palestine. This was the natural path for me to follow, that I would not make my life in America but would go to Palestine to make my life as a Jew, and I got here in 1946."

• "My father came to America in 1906 and tried to study agriculture in preparation for going to Palestine," said another teacher. "My family looked on America as a way station. My father became a professional Zionist, but it bothered me that he never did manage to get to Palestine. It disturbed me. But *I* got here, finally, in 1950."

These were migrants, then, who were realizing a life's goal set before them from childhood, often realizing it where their fathers had failed. To this drive has to be added all the ideological and emotional commitment generated by their political groups, and the fact that even among their political comrades, they were an elite minority who finally "made aliya," that is, actually left America to take part in the winning of the Land of Israel, a small epic in itself in which a person got the rare chance to have his own finest hour. It is therefore not difficult to guess, perhaps even to assume, that for many of them the parting from America had less sorrow or ambivalence in it, and the commitment of their tomorrows to their chosen new land many fewer reservations or hesitations. Even so, many of these heavily motivated young pioneers apparently failed to stay with their commitment—again, one gets various unverifiable figures on this, but it is commonly said that for every one that stayed at least two left, some leaving the kibbutz for the town, some leaving to quit Israel altogether and to return home to America. But it is among the survivors of this strongly oriented group, brought up on Zionism, molded by political ideologies and commitments, and held together by strong group sanctions and the shared memory of their great toil and devotion to this cause, that one now finds the most settled and relatively the most integrated American Jews in Israel.

Besides early Zionist conditioning, the other great spur to migration to Israel by Americans was the fate of Europe's Jews at the hands of Hitler. I met some individuals who had strayed from the early Zionist path but were brought back to it by the holocaust and its aftermath. Such a one was a tall, graying, weary man of about forty, born and raised in Pittsburgh, whose devotion to his job as a government servant in Israel for about ten years had worn him thin and dogged. "I see myself so differently now from the way I saw myself then that I wonder how one ever gets to understand these things anyway," he said with a tired smile. "My family was Zionist. This gave it a negative value for me when I was younger. I didn't become Zionist or even particularly Jewish until the war. I was trained in the Air Force as a navigator but worked as a statistician because of my skill in math. We began to hear what was happening to the Jews in Europe. By the time I was out of the service and had gone to Columbia to get a Ph.D., what was happening in Europe was affecting me greatly. I could have finished in 1948 and gotten an assistant professorship, but when the war broke out in Israel, I decided to come and help build this state."

Another was a former Boston lawyer, now principal of a high school on a kibbutz. "My father came to America from Russia in 1908, a devout Zionist. He knew Hebrew, he believed in the Zionist ideal, but he lived in America in perfect comfort. He did not attempt to rationalize it. I really started out myself as a non-Zionist. In 1937, my parents sent me to Palestine for one year, but when it was over I went back, went to law school, and into law practice. During the war I worked for the [U.S.] government, satisfying myself with a whole series of rationalizations. It took me until 1948, practicing law all that time with my father, to decide on the validity of Jewish nationalism and socialism. It was a time of dramatic struggle. I do not know

what would have happened to me if it had not been for
the external situation. When I decided to go to Palestine in 1948, I was thirty-three. I wasn't much of a
fighter, I must say, but I almost did get killed in the
fighting we had around here, and I guess that qualifies
me."

But there were many who came to Israel at this
period who had been only faintly brushed earlier in
their lives by Zionism or not at all. Many had been
raised with some elementary Jewish education or expo-
sure to religious observance, but there were others who
did not even have this much content in their Jewishness when they were jolted by the discovery of what
had happened to six million Jews in Hitler's Europe,
and in some cases even more by the West's failure, and
especially the American failure, to bring timely succor
to the victims or to give refuge afterwards to the survivors. This experience deepened the sense of Jewish
identification and separateness among surviving Jews
everywhere, including those in America. Americans,
almost all veterans of the war, enlisted in the Aliya
Beth, the forces helping to carry out the "illegal immigration," smuggling Jews out of Europe, manning ten
of the ships that ran the British blockade in the Medi-
terranean between 1945 and 1948. With the procla-
mation of the State and the beginning of the war
against the Arab states, another foreign brigade, called
the Mahal—from the Hebrew initials for Overseas
Volunteer Brigade—was hastily recruited to take part.

Of its 5,300 men, 1,770 were Americans, who formed whole units and played crucial roles as officers, especially in the Air Force—one American unit lost 30 percent of its officers during the short but rough war fought against heavy numerical odds to win and keep the new state. According to a report of a poll taken among themselves, 98 percent of them were veterans of the American armed services, 95 percent were unaffiliated to any Zionist organization, 90 percent of them knew no Hebrew when they arrived, 85 percent knew no Yiddish either, 83 percent of them were American-born, and only 3 percent of them said that they had thought of settling in Israel after the war. According to this source, 370 American veterans of the Aliya Beth and the Mahal did actually in the end remain or return as settlers.[*]

"We debate on why we came," said one of the members of this migration, "whether out of Zionism, or out of religion. I don't know. I'm not orthodox. There was no Zionism in my family. I was in the army for three years during the war, was in the Philippines, and I was there when I learned of the plight of European Jews. I was disappointed in the non-Jewish world, in the view it took of the Jewish plight. I came to feel my Jewishness more than my Americanism. I came in 1948."

An energetic young man who was born in the Bronx and whose father, an immigrant from Poland, washed

[*] Lapide, *A Century of U.S. Aliya,* pp. 91, 95–96.

windows for a living, had served as an officer in the American merchant marine during the war. "There was nothing Zionist in my life, no Zionist youth movement, nothing. When I got out in 1946, I began to read about the situation. When I heard about the call for volunteers for the illegal immigration ships, I decided to find out about it. I asked only one question: was it for pay or for no pay. They said it was for no pay, and I said, OK, I'll go. If people were going to be paid, they could find better-qualified people than me, and I wasn't interested. But if it's a volunteer deal, I said, OK, I'd go. That was the beginning of my Zionism. Why? How do we know? There was what happened in Europe and what didn't happen. It's what the Nazis did and what the democratic countries didn't do. I'm a Jew, maybe I ought to put that first in explaining why. I really don't know where that fits. Then there's the fact that I was brought up in the American tradition, whatever that is. To me it means you're for the underdog, and these Jews were really the underdogs."

Neither a Zionist upbringing nor the shock of the holocaust could obviously be the whole explanation for an individual's act of migration. There were many more Jews who shared in these experiences who did not go to Israel. There is no question, however, that for those who did go, especially during the critical and dangerous period of reclaiming the land, of struggle for the state, the illegal immigration, and the war with the Arabs, these drives did provide substance, sharpness, and the sources of much-needed stamina. It was a time for heroes, and even the least among them could live the rest of his life on the emotional capital generated by that finest hour of commitment. "Me, I can say I participated in creating the Jewish state, a homeland for Jews," said one of them, "that's what *we* did, I mean those who came to fight or to take part in the kibbutz movement before the war. The guy who came after all of that can't say as much. I'll also say that my kids won't get out of this what I've gotten out of it."

For most of those who came afterwards, in the 1950s and since, it was all a much blurrier matter, both in their reasons for coming and their experience after they came. If it was out of Zionism or an earlier Zionist background, it was a steeply refracted Zionism, no longer easily defined and much embattled both in Israel and America where Zionists have not even until now redefined themselves in the light of the reality of the Jewish state. Hardly anybody comes to Israel any more to become an agricultural pioneer or even less to build some kind of Zionist-socialist Utopian society in the Holy Land of the Jews. The Hitler holocaust has its place in the mind of every Jew of this generation, although its jaggedness is already so flattened out by the onrolling years that the Israeli leadership felt impelled through the Eichmann trial a few years ago to remind their own young people and the rest of the world of what had happened. Hardly any American Jew in Israel would say he migrated because—as some Zionists still darkly prophesy—it could happen again, and in America too. In the early 1950s a few politically motivated American migrants did come, to get away from McCarthyism or the Korean War or both. But the fear that America was about to be made over in the image of McCarthy (plus Cohn and Schine) quickly passed and the Korean War also came to an end at about the same time. By far the greater number of migrants of these last ten years or so have been middle-class American Jews whose dissatisfactions with their lives in America were much vaguer. They came to Israel to satisfy some need they felt as Jews—to fill some lack they felt as Jews in America—but it seems fair to say that most of them hoped, while solving the problems of their Jewishness, to reproduce as far as possible in Israel the way of life they had enjoyed at home in America. For many of them this was more than a matter of material comforts; it touched deeper values as well.

In the explanations I was given for the "push" and the "pull" involved in leaving America and coming to Israel, two formulas most frequently recurred. One was the oddly jarring statement: "By coming to Israel I solved the Jewish question." The second was the more positive though vague affirmation: "I came to Israel to lead the full Jewish life."

"Solving the Jewish question" sounded at first hearing disconcertingly like certain similar phrases—"final solution" was the one that kept coming into my mind —and this impression was not dispelled by some of the first answers that came to my further questions. "I mean that being here you don't have to define your Jewishness," answered a university professor somewhat shortly. "That question is removed." What was actually being removed was made a bit clearer by another intellectual: "Here you don't think of being a Jew. It's no problem. You don't think of it all the time as I did when I was a kid, that I was somehow different, subtly or otherwise. One was always conscious of it." A kibbutznik, who was no intellectual at all, gave this feeling a literal, almost physical quality when he described his sensations upon returning to the United States for a visit. "The only place I never felt like a Jew was here in Israel," he said. "When I got off the ship in New York, I knew. As soon as I got off the ship, I felt like a Jew again." And when I asked him what it was he felt, he replied: "I would be particularly concerned when I was with non-Jews, I wouldn't yell too much, or use my hands too much." A young man who also said that what he liked about being in Israel was that he did "not have to think of being Jewish" went on to say: "In the United States the question about being Jewish is always on your mind, as to what difference it makes. You wonder how *they* feel. You have to be careful and watch out. Here you feel really at ease." Or again, more explicitly still: "Here you don't feel you have to be on your best behavior, that you have to make a good impression, worry about being accepted. In America, you go to a party, you size up with whom you can talk freely and with whom you can't tell jokes, let your hair down. Here I am much more at ease. There, there was the Jewish crowd and the non-Jewish crowd. Here, there are just Jews. Jews in the States try to achieve this themselves, congregating in Jewish resorts, associations, fraternities, and so on. No, I wouldn't say I was unhappy in the States, just had a heightened awareness of the inherent unwillingness of the Gentile community to accept Jews. I was back there last month and I put myself on my best behavior, like somebody from a foreign country, watching what I said. . . ."*

One of the fullest and most explicit statements of this unease in the Gentile world came from the only authentic working-class type I met among the Zionist Socialists on the kibbutzim I visited, a hard-muscled man who had come to Israel from Brooklyn ten years before. He said:

"There was no getting away from being a Jew in America. I wasn't ashamed of being a Jew, but then

---

* Or, as a character in *The Victim,* an early Saul Bellow novel, says: "You couldn't say you were master of yourself when there were so many people by whom you could be humiliated."

maybe I was. I don't know. But there would be a
thousand small subtle things, nothing really tough. It'd
be easy if somebody called you a Jew bastard or something, and you let go and fight it out. It was all the
other things. You get a job in a place and you come in
and the meet the other guys and the first question,
mind you, the first question, not what's your name or
where do you come from, but *what are you?* So I'd say
I'm a sheenie and what're you going to make out of it?
Calm down, he says, don't get het up, it's all right with
me. And maybe it is and maybe it isn't. I became a
bowler, the best bowler in the shop, and used to go all
around with our bowling team, but always it was being
different from the others in some way. Once when I
was a kid we moved to a small town upstate and the
priest came by and invited us to come to his church.
No, we says, we're Jews. The Protestant minister came
and invited us to his church. And we say, no thank you,
we're Jews, and he said, come anyway. The Catholics
and Protestants were fighting in that town and my
mother said to me: keep away from all of them, we're
different from them. Or we walk down the street with
our girl and a woman says, now there you are, a perfect
colleen of a girl, the perfect colleen. And my wife says,
no, she's not a colleen, she's Jewish. I don't know, it's
hard to describe, but it was like a thousand small nails,
each one a nail in your back. Here you're away from all
that."

And here, finally the same theme as it was struck by

another kibbutz veteran who was schooled at the University of Minnesota:

"Although some of my best friends are Goyim, there is never any doubt that I am I and they are they. I did not want to subject myself or my children to this ever-so-small but permanent conflict, the awareness of not being 100 percent at home. For example in a class at college you could discuss any subject under the sun with complete freedom, yet when you got home among your Jewish fellows, there was still always greater freedom. There is always some kind of imperceptible restraint. Go to a Jewish lodge and bring one non-Jew in, and you find an imperceptible change in the presence of a Goy. You sit up a little straighter, you talk a wee bit more grammatically, you will be a wee bit more polite. It's true. If you called this to the attention of those concerned, they would be offended and deny it. The Goy might not even be aware of it. But I would be. It's the difference between the in-group and the out-group. It was not a question of friction. What is relevant is a feeling of being at ease. Why couldn't we feel at ease? If I weren't a twentieth-century rationalist, I would say it was historic memory, memory of the Spanish Inquisition, of the Russian persecutions, of Hitler. Historic memory is there. But I am more or less of a rationalist. I'm not given to mystiques. Still I will say this is something that passes from generation to generation. As people say: 'When all is said and done, the world of the Goy, don't trust it.' "

For these individuals, it seems clear, "solving the Jewish question" did not have anything to do with defining their Jewishness; it had to do with getting away from the Gentiles. It meant moving out from under the real or imagined superiority, rejection, or hostility of the Gentiles and coming to live in a Jewish state where everybody or nearly everybody was a Jew. This was the refuge, the relief, the pleasure, the satisfaction, the one thing each person could say he had gained. As one said: "There is one thing we have all got. Everybody's gotten the one basic desire. Here we are all Jews together." And this, for many, was a good and sufficient—if incomplete—definition of the "full Jewish life." It meant, for one thing, being able to relax and be one's own Jewish self, whatever that might be. "In America," explained an older settler, "you were always trying to be a 'good' Jew. Here *everything* you do is Jewish." It meant, along one important dimension, being part at last of a majority instead of forever being in a minority. This meant substituting a Jewish pecking order for a Gentile pecking order, confronting Gentile "outsiders" at last as Jewish "insiders," and for some it meant, most of all, facing Gentile hostility with Jewish power. The Jewish state might, like the ghetto, exist rimmed by foes, but while the ghetto's walls fenced in fear, submission, and helplessness, the state's boundaries could bristle with armed defensiveness. As the muscular man from Brooklyn put it "I hate to say it, it sounds terrible, but

I'll say it anyway. Here you can meet all that, if you have to, with a gun."

Although all of this could and did provide some satisfactions, some answers with which some people could be content, it still left unanswered the questions about what it might now come to mean to be a "Jew" and to live something called "the full Jewish life" in Israel. These are prime questions now for all the Jews in Israel—and elsewhere as well—but for the Americans there they assume their own special and peculiar forms. Their answers were wrapped up in each person's idea of what it meant to be an American and a Jew and in each person's way of wrestling with the confusion and ambiguity dominating both halves of this double identity. These were some of the more deeply gnawing problems of life, the source of that "private agony" which so many of these Americans carried with them as they wrestled as manfully as they could day after day with the even more numerous and sometimes more aggravating problems of living in Israel.

5. Problems of Living

"Almost all Americans who come here," said an American old-timer, "come out of high idealistic motives and they conjure up a perfect Israel, and consequently they come down with a big bump."

The bump comes in different ways and in different places for different people. The reasons they have for coming to Israel have much to do with what Americans do and where they go and what happens to them after they get there. Those who have come through the various Zionist youth organizations have usually come explicitly as recruits for one of the kibbutzim and they move out directly onto that path of experience of living in Israel, with all its unique attractions and all its unique disabilities, especially for individualist Americans trying to become collectivists. These communal recruits, never a large number, have become fewer still in recent years. As already indicated, much the greater number of American migrants who have come since the founding of the State have come as individuals to make their way on their own and have mostly moved into the cities, seeking places for themselves in urban occupations. The kibbutzniks and the urban dwellers share in one degree or another most of the fundamental problems of life that face American Jews in Israel, but their problems of living are quite different. Except for some of the newer and most exposed places, the early rigor and hardship and danger of kibbutz life have been giving way in recent years to a somewhat more secure and more comfortable stability. Whatever the problems American kibbutzniks have to cope with, they do not lie in the areas of low wages and high costs, scarce and expensive housing, language, schooling for children, and the bureaucratic miasmas of many different kinds with which newly come urban-dwelling migrants must wrestle so desperately in their efforts to become settled settlers. For these new arrivals, these bumps come in a great variety of shapes and sizes and make the going very rough for many from the very beginning, often in the process of arrival.

Israel has developed assembly-line techniques for receiving and absorbing immigrants in masses who come by the shipload in "forced" migrations from various places. It has none, however, for receiving individuals who come in "free aliya," that is, as immigrants coming of their own free choice, especially Americans who are all assumed to be "rich" and therefore to need no assistance from anybody. It is the most commonly heard complaint of American settlers that although Israeli Zionist authorities keep saying they want to attract Western and especially American immigrants, not enough is done to help them or even to recognize that they have special needs. Some special provisions are made in a few cases for specially qualified professionals who are recruited for certain jobs in Israel and come on contracts which take care of most of their essential requirements, but there is nothing of this kind for the much larger number of more ordinary people who belong to no organizations and find that they are left very painfully on their own. These Americans are in the worst way in this respect, for while the other "Anglo-Saxons" from England or South Africa have strong support from sponsoring organizations at home, the great majority of American immigrants do not. The small Zionist youth groups naturally support only their own recruits, and the larger American Zionist movement remains largely indifferent to them, American migration to Israel being a touchy subject that deeply divides American and Israeli Zionists. This is what leads some American migrants to Israel to see themselves as "orphans." They feel that no one at home in America supports them and that no one in Israel seems to care what happens to them. They are left to make their own way through the mazes of the formidable Israeli bureaucracy and the stringencies of the Israeli job and housing markets and to fight their own way through the struggle to get themselves settled. The Association of Americans and Canadians in Israel, created for the purpose, has been trying as best it could to supply some of the help most of them badly need, but for most American newcomers in Israel, getting settled has usually been a long and trying experience.

Problems of living in Israel is one subject that has been rather well covered in the writing one can find by and about American Jews in Israel. To a remarkable extent much the same things were being reported by sympathetic writers a dozen years ago, five years ago, and in the last year or so, and were being repeated in published interviews by spokesmen for the American group of settlers and would-be settlers.* For this reason, although I spent many hours listening to details of this kind, and although they are an extremely important part of the story—for many the decisive one—I do not feel the need to dwell at length upon them here, but only to indicate some of the main features as they were described to me at the time of my visit.

There was first for all newcomers the acute problem of language. Some Americans of mature age find mastery of Hebrew extremely difficult to achieve and this alone keeps them in some degree apart not only from much of Israeli life but also, in due time, from their own children who grow up speaking the new tongue and who may at best acquire an approximate English as a second language. For those who come

* Cf. Hal Lehrman, "When Americans Emigrate to Israel," *Commentary,* February, 1952; Eliezer Whartman, "Why So Small an Aliyah from America," *The Reconstructionist,* March 7, 1952; Alvin Rosenfeld, "Americans in Israel," New York *Herald Tribune,* June 12–18, 1961; "Seeds from the West," *Jerusalem Post Weekly,* January 1, 1965; Ronald Sanders, "Settling in Israel?" *Commentary,* August, 1965; "An American Zionist Tells Why She's Going Back," *Jerusalem Post,* September 12, 1966.

with children of school age, both the language problem and the shortage of adequate schools become gravely pressing matters—there is as yet no universal or free public schooling available past the primary levels, only half of the eligible age group is actually in the high schools that do exist, the competition for places is keen and the American child who is a relative latecomer to the environment is likely to be at a severe disadvantage. Again, in the matter of jobs, much of the difficulty experienced by many newcomers stems from some of the hard facts of Israeli economic life. There are places for individuals at high levels of specialized technical or administrative skill, but it is much harder for the more normally endowed or trained individual to find where he can fit in. Doctors, teachers, and community service professionals of various kinds can find useful work to do if they can solve the language problem, manage at the available salary scales, and are willing to rough it in one of the "new towns" or outlying areas where new immigrants are being located. Lawyers have to find something else they can do if they want to do it in Israel. In the jobs that they can find and fill, Americans can hope to earn salaries that are about one-third or less of what they might expect to earn at home. A typical upper-level take-home paycheck (the tax deductions are heavy) would be equivalent to about $250 or $300 a month, while the cost of living is not anywhere near that much below the level at home. It is roughly accurate to say that a move for such an American to Israel means cutting his standard of living by about a third.

The most grinding of the more purely economic difficulties have to do with housing. There is almost no rental housing available and the cost of buying small and generally inadequate apartments is cruelly high. One of the best-situated Americans I met, a highly placed government official, brings home just about $300 a month. His small two-bedroom apartment had cost about £16,000 or about $5,300, some seven years before. With the arrival of another child, his family needed more space, and since property values had rocketed in Jerusalem, their apartment could now bring in £30,000 or£35,000 and this seemed an enormous sum to them until they went looking and saw nothing they would accept that cost less than £50,000 or £60,000—$15,000 to $20,000, a sum astronomically out of sight as far as they were concerned. The Jewish Agency makes long-term low-interest loans to masses of immigrants who move into the huge apartment blocks provided for them, but these are of a kind that no American immigrant would be likely to be willing to live in and most of them are located in places where he does not want to go. For apartments that he will make do with—and these are very rarely equivalent even to the most modest kind of living spaces he could expect to have at home—he has to pay these much higher prices and without the help of mortgage funds available in the ordinary way to which he is accustomed. In a country where all capital is being poured into development enterprise, little or none is available for private housing. I was told that one could sometimes get a mortgage loan equivalent to perhaps 25 percent of the value of the property at a rate of 10 percent per annum. The Association of Americans and Canadians in Israel had been struggling to raise a mortgage fund of its own and it has been instrumental in building several housing projects designed for Americans, but these efforts have not come close to meeting the need. During 1965, the Jewish Agency offered to make available 500 apartments that might be more acceptable to Americans, 40 of them in Jerusalem, the rest in Tel Aviv, Beersheba, and several other places. The plan was to offer them for a deposit of $1,000 on a 2½-room (plus kitchen) apartment, with rentals equivalent to about $30 to $35 a month, with the deposit applicable at a future date, if desired, on a purchase at a probable price of £30,000, or $10,000. Desirable apartments in Tel Aviv run up to £60,000 and £80,000 and in a block of luxury apartments newly built in Jerusalem—where, as a pioneering early immigrant scornfully informed me, "they are going to have a doorman!"—apartments were going for £90,000. Very few "rich" Americans who could afford any of these prices are by way of becoming settlers in Israel. A would-be settler, I was told in 1963 (and conditions have hardly improved in 1966), should come to the country with no less than $10,000 to see him and his family through the initial period of learning Hebrew while living in an *ulpan* (a combined boardinghouse and language school) , getting enough of the language to start shopping around for work, getting settled in some kind of job and beginning to earn, and—if any is left and with terribly good luck— to help toward buying some first small place to live. A small businessman who comes hoping to open some kind of small shop or buy into some small business will not get very far with less than $50,000 and he will not get very far with that much. "What is $50,000 in a place where the new tendency is toward supermarkets and department stores?" asked one of my informants. "The pastoral dream of a Zionist Israel has been disrupted by the need for quick industrialization with all its rapid pace and its inequalities and problems." But whether it is $10,000 or $50,000, such sums, he indicated, "are for the initial haul only. Money gives out quickly, things are expensive and many people can't stretch what they have or bring in more funds soon enough. They can't make it and they have to give up."

Almost as rough as the stories of housing hardships are the accounts one hears of coping with the Israeli bureaucracy, which is apparently like all bureaucracies, only much, much more so. This struggle begins almost from the first hour of arrival and goes on for months and even for years, over problems of bringing things in through customs, over permits of various kinds, papers relating to housing, jobs, taxes, and status, and all the many other points at which an individual meets not only the government in semisocialist Israel, but also the quasi-government bureaus of the Jewish Agency with which he must deal in many of the most essential matters of his everyday existence. "Americans coming here with their idealistic expectations find out that Jews are people too," said a veteran settler, "people with all their petty foibles. They find that they are not angels. They also find the bureaucracy and the general lack of efficiency so different from what they feel they are used to. Here you get so much more closely involved with the government. Everything is so small and so close and you are much more in contact with it. They don't answer the telephones very well and often they will keep people waiting while they are drinking tea and they are not polite. It is probably the same as other bureaucracies, I just don't know, but you might spend a whole day just getting a signature on a piece of paper and you might have to go to many different offices to get it done." Thirteen years ago one reporter found American immigrants in Israel "furious over Israeli indifference, rudeness, political favoritism,"* and when I checked (in 1963) on some of the most highly aggravating details of the "bureaucratic runaround" I heard from both newcomers and old-timers, I got some helpless shrugs from officials at the Jewish Agency. The then executive director of the Association, which has been fighting the battle of the bureaucracy from the beginning, nodded wearily and said: "Yes, that's the way it is. Runaround *is* the sys-

* Hal Lehrman, loc. cit.

tem. I have one example in my file of somebody who had to go to 43 different offices over many weeks to do something he had to do. There are some terrible stories." More recently still, the president of the association publicly complained about the way immigrants had "to run from one office to the other" and she called them "hair-raising stories."*

There is sometimes more than mere bureaucratic sluggishness or petty tyrannizing in some of this, for some of the treatment received by Americans is apparently due to the fact that they *are* Americans. This is partly because Americans usually present the bureaucrat with problems different from those he has to meet from other Israelis, and this is sufficiently upsetting and irritating in itself. There is besides this, however, a certain aggravating factor of prejudice in the encounter. Americans do enjoy a measure of status and prestige in Israel, but they pay a price for it. "You know, Israelis are jealous and envious about Americans," explained one longtime warrior in these battles, "and they approach Americans not as Jews but as Americans, with all the stereotypes attached about being rich and so on. There are all kinds of difficulties and unpleasant things." He paused and looked at me a little speculatively. "Still, you know," he said, "we are still all Jews, and we try and shelter these things, some of the facts. Nobody writes critical pieces about Israel. People wouldn't believe it, and anyway, to things like this the Israeli answer is: 'We have bigger problems.

* *Jerusalem Post,* loc. cit.

We're only fifteen years old. Look at all the things we *are* doing!'

"Many Americans," he went on, "can't give up the American style. They miss too many things too much. But I think this only happens if other things happen first. I mean that all kinds of other difficulties pile up and begin to get them down. A man comes here feeling like a hero, he is going to devote himself to Israel and so on, but then all this comes on him and he begins to weaken, and it gets tougher, and then finally comes a point where he simply can't take another one. That one comes, and it is just too much."

We were sitting at an open café on a street in Tel Aviv, and at this moment in our conversation, a recent American newcomer came bounding toward us across the street. He was one of those from whom I had freshly heard a long but calm and highly factual account of the newcomer's problems, the customs, learning the language, the place he had to live in, the school his daughter had to go to—but now his face was shining. "I've broken the ice!" he shouted as he came up. G——, the man I was sitting with, had put him on to a chance to earn some money selling encyclopedias, and he had just sold his first set, entirely on his own, and it had transformed his immediate world by making it seem possible that he would be able to live in it. The two talked over some business details and the radiantly transformed salesman went on his way.

"He's a good type," said G——, "and not too usual.

Too many others come with stars in their eyes, no feet on the ground, and they are not really prepared for what they find here. All they have is what they've been told by the Jewish Agency propaganda which sold them on the idea of coming to Israel. But Z—— knows better, he takes an honest approach, and if more people came with his attitude, they might make out better. And this is what I keep telling them, I give them the worst. Lots of people don't like the way I talk. I say you're not going to be a hero doing this. Nobody here wants you. If you think Israel needs *you,* nothing doing, you're a fool, don't come, stay away. But do *you* need Israel? That's the question. If you think you need Israel, then come, and do whatever you have to do in order to satisfy your need. That's the way to make it."

Many have not made it, as the figures show, but quite a few have. For those who manage, with stamina and some luck, to stick, these problems of living either subside or become a way of life, part of the price to be paid for the satisfactions to be gained by staying on. But along with these satisfactions, whatever they may be for any of these would-be migrants, they must also shoulder all the other burdens of their choice, and these have to do not so much with these problems of living in Israel, grievous as they are, but with a great tangle of problems of life there, which are more formidable still.

6. Being "Americans"

When they tried to describe the satisfactions of their lives as settlers in Israel, the American Jews I talked to there usually fell back on one or more of a fairly common set of formulas. The most common:

"Here I am a Jew among Jews." Or: *"Here the whole culture is Jewish."* Or: *"Here I can lead a Jewish life."*

Another satisfaction named by some was the feeling that by taking part in the re-creation of the Jewish state of Israel, they were living to some higher purpose, giving importance to their lives in ways they could not hope to realize if they had held to the more purely privatistic goals they would have pursued had they remained home in America. *"We are taking part here, life has more meaning here."*

There was, finally, a feeling that for some made all the difficulties seem minor by comparison to the greatest gain of all: "My little spot here is incomparably less comfortable than any place I would live in America," said a kibbutz veteran, *"but this is mine."*

It would take much greater and more intimate knowledge than I could have about anyone I met in Israel to be able to show how any particular person struck his own balance among these pluses and minuses; this is each man's unique story. The American Jews I encountered would doubtless arrange themselves in some kind of order along these dimensions of "satisfaction" or, if you will, "happiness." I certainly met some who looked and sounded happy and others who did not look or sound happy at all: I have no scale by which to measure this most intangible of intangibles. What I could do was try my best to pursue each person's answers into the maze of multiplying complications, dilemmas, and further questions into which they led. This was a labyrinth into which each individual would take me only as far as his tolerance of my questions and his temperament would allow him to go. I could not presume to plumb the experience of any one person; I could only listen to what he said and try to relate it to what others said. I met some individuals who seemed to stay happy by keeping out of the maze altogether. I met others who had gone deeply into it, and while they were not happy about being in it, would not be happy anywhere else. There were those, finally, who were plainly and explicitly and quite verbally unhappy. I repeat: it is neither my task nor my intent to try to arrive at judgments of this kind, either about any single individual or about the group. I am interested rather in trying to sort out those aspects of their common experience which come upon these American Jews in Israel precisely because they *are* American, and to see how their identity as *Americans* imposes itself on their attempt to define their identity as *Jews* in Israel.

The sensation of being a *Jew among Jews* holds only for as long as one can go on seeing all Jews as a great undifferentiated mass. This seems most possible at the beginning, perhaps most strongly of all at the actual time of arrival when a Jew come to Zion can feel washed over with the total presence of other Jews and all things "Jewish." As I listened to some individuals describe how they felt on coming into a place where "everybody is a Jew and everything is Jewish," I remembered it as the sensation identically experienced by American Negroes in West Africa on coming to a place where everyone is black.* In both cases, some of

* Compare two passages, the first from a story about an English Jewish visitor arriving in Israel: "What made us forget the bad weather . . . was the Hebrew. There were signs in Hebrew, advertisements in Hebrew, the wording on the officials' hats was Hebrew, the radio blared in Hebrew, the porters cursed in Hebrew, and the policemen, soldiers and sailors and taxi-drivers were Hebrews."—Shalom Namali, "There's a Stranger Close Behind Us," in "Israel Seen From Within," a special issue of the *Jewish Frontier,* December, 1964.

The second is from my own report on Negro Americans in West Africa: "On first arriving almost anywhere in West Africa now, an American Negro visitor feels a tingling thrill to see black men everywhere, black men doing all the jobs, lowly *and* high, right up to the black men who now sit in the seats of power. . . . He feels a great relieving pleasure wash over him at the loss of conspicuousness in a black crowd. 'It gave me a sort of joy,' said a young man from the Midwest. 'On the streets, the billboards with black faces, and, most of all, that great sea of black faces the day I went to the stadium.' "—*The New World of Negro Americans,* p. 303.

What is even more striking about these two passages, however, are the sentences with which each one continues. The story about the English this satisfaction lasts. A Jew in a world without Gentiles and a Negro in a world without whites can feel relieved of that "uneasiness"—really fear—which the Gentile or white presence creates. As we have already suggested, being a "Jew among Jews" was a way of ceasing to be a Jew, or at least ceasing to be the "Jew" as object of Gentile rejection and anti-Semitism. To be sure, this could—and for many did—also mean that a person was finally able, in all-Jewish Israel, to measure himself and others not as "Jews" but as individual persons. Some of this took place as an important personal experience. "It was my temperament to idealize," said an older American kibbutznik speaking of his younger years, "and in practice I had to learn that Jews are also human beings, that they act petty, pretty much the same wherever they are." This might seem an unduly complicated way of having an elementary maturing experience but what it meant was that in Israel one could cease at last to be *special* because one was Jewish. But what happened, ironically enough, was that one now became *special* because one was *American*. The undifferentiated mass sorted itself out into its many different parts, not only different kinds of human beings who happen to be Jews, but also

---

Jewish visitor goes on: "One felt comfortable and at home, with even the slight feeling of superiority for being English as well." And of the Negro in West Africa: "Yet almost at once this young man's sensation became mixed. He did not want to get quite so lost. . . . 'I really wanted to be seen not as an African but as an American . . . I wanted to be understood to be an American.'"

different kinds of Jews, each with a different history and a different character. It was one of the most commonly remarked features of the experience—again almost identical to that described by American Negroes in West Africa: "In America," said a woman settler, "I was a Jew, but here when people think of me, they think of me as an American. Here we are not all Israelis together, but we are Americans living in Israel." To be *American*, it turned out, was to be clearly distinct from all the others in many important ways.

"Orphans"

There is, to begin with, the feeling that some Americans in Israel have that they are "orphans" who do not belong anywhere to anybody. This was not the feeling of American kibbutzniks more or less snugly attached to their own special organizations in America and much more deeply rooted in their communes in Israel. It was found, rather, among the much larger number of unattached American urban settlers or would-be settlers who saw themselves as the unacknowledged children of Zionism in America and uncared-for interlopers in Israel. Indeed, I heard much stronger language used by the incoming president of the Association of Americans and Canadians in Israel in the spring of 1963, an earnestly serious man named Meier

Kaplan, who had abandoned the study of philosophy
for the study of criminology and police methods and
had become a high official of the police establishment
in Israel. In his inaugural speech, Kaplan likened
Americans and Canadians in Israel to "bastards" who,
he reminded his audience, were excluded by Holy
Writ from the assembly of God, "even unto the tenth
generation." Their roots, he said, were "anomalous as
far as roots are concerned." "We were not formed by
the act of any Zionist organization in America or
Canada," he said, "nor were we formed by the veteran
settlers from America and Canada who preceded us
here before the formation of the State of Israel. We
were not formed by any political party in Israel. We
formed ourselves," he cried, "springing out of no-
where, without legitimacy. One of the poignant minor
themes of our association was the search for a parent,
for roots, for legitimacy, for identification with a specific past."* During the rest of the meeting, the same
plaintively orphaned note was struck again and again.
The executive secretary's report dealt largely with
the dogged efforts of the Association to get recognition
from officialdom in Israel and from the major Zionist
groups in America, the one still failing to meet the
special needs of the individual and voluntary immigration of Americans and Canadians and the latter,
caught up in the complications of Israel-American

* *Bulletin of the AACI*, April–May, 1963, p. 3.

Zionist relations, offering no help of any kind to Americans who did migrate. But if it was bad not to be able to say who their "parents" were, it was much worse still not to be able to identify themselves. This deeper, more painful nerve, was touched by a writer in the *Bulletin* a year earlier:

> Let us face it, many of our members have not clarified their own attitudes and still wonder: Are we Americans-Canadians in Israel or are we Israelis formerly of North America? Are our former compatriots in North America utter strangers (except those who happen to be our relatives) who should merely "send us money" and not bother us? Are we ourselves some superior breed—superior to our former compatriots in that we have left "the fleshpots" and superior to our present compatriots in that we decided of our own free will to share their burden?*

Settlers by Choice

It was, indeed, an almost uniquely distinctive fact about American Jewish settlers in Israel that they had come not out of necessity but by their own choice. This was also true, though with a certain difference, of the other "Anglo-Saxons"—English, Australian, South African, and some West Europeans. Because they had come freely, many Americans tell you, Israelis tend to look upon them as either super-idealists or super-fools,

* *Bulletin of the AACI*, March–April, 1962, p. 4.

or often as both. As most admiringly seen by some Israelis, the act of "free" migration links the Americans in spirit with the earlier Zionist pioneers, a spirit not much in evidence now in the greater mass of present-day Israelis, most of whom came to Israel in flight from Hitlerian or post-Hitlerian Europe and from Moslem hostility in North Africa and the Near and Middle East. Admiration for high idealism, like high idealism itself, has severe limits at best, however, and in the atmosphere of what is called "normalization" in Israel now, it is not likely to be carried very far. Most of the time, in any case, the "free migration" of the Americans is not admiringly seen at all. For one thing, the difference is not always an acknowledged one. "No Israeli really admits he came here without a choice," observed one American. "Everybody feels he had a choice and chose Israel as a voluntary act." With or without this added element of self-deception, many such Israelis will commonly argue that Americans really have no choice either, this American went on, "warning in one breath that anti-Semitism is going to wipe out all the Jews in America, and saying in the next breath that assimilation was going to do it." There are many Israelis who would have much preferred—and still prefer—refuge in the United States rather than in Israel, and for many of them, a person has to be out of his mind to choose to leave the secure comforts of big America and take on the insecure discomforts of little Israel. Many an American, fighting his daily battle against frustration, often finds himself thinking the same thing.

But there are several things about the American's freedom of choice which touch in sensitive ways on the quality of his relations with Israelis. It means, for one thing, that besides being able to come freely, he can also leave freely. Unlike most people in Israel, he has a place to go back to if he wants to go. If things get too rough, or he changes his mind, he can pick up and leave, and he has often done so. For this limit on his commitment he is both criticized and envied. But there is something in this that cuts more deeply still, for the American has a home and family back there, people, kinfolk, connections, something many of the present adult generation of European immigrants in Israel no longer have. Sometimes feeling about the difference crops out only at the shallower levels—e.g., resentment and controversy on the kibbutzim over gifts Americans get from home. ("We were looked upon as spoiled Americans who wouldn't stick it out anyway. We came with some things, household things, and they were envious of us.") But sometimes—as I heard from some who spoke of it with an almost guilty sadness—it becomes a challenge to which there is no answer: "One woman actually said to me once: 'It's so unfair! Your children have two sets of grandparents and ours have *none!*' " The Americans are still intact in ways that many European Israelis are not, and this makes them "rich Americans" in ways

that separate them far more than the simpler forms of
their greater affluence.

"Rich Americans"

To be sure, this simpler kind of "rich American"
figures prominently in the standard set of hostile stereotypes that govern Israeli prejudices against Americans.
These are applied to America and Americans in general, whether as part of the universal response of the
weak to the strong, beneficiary to benefactor, or as a
reflection of the dislike or distrust of American world
policy behavior, especially in relation to the Arab
countries and Israel. They are also more especially
applied to American Jews, who are most generally seen
as rich Jews who think they can discharge their obligations to Israel simply by giving money and who are
represented most directly by the tourists who swarm
into Israel from America each year. Much of this rubs
off, finally, on the American Jews who come to Israel to
stay, who have to take all the slings and arrows thrown
at America in the large and American Jews in general
as well as a few aimed at them in particular.

"Yes, there are prejudices against Americans," said a
veteran American city-dwelling settler. "There is the
feeling of the rich uncle. The average Israeli sees the
American Jew as a giver of gifts, and this entails a
picture of the Israeli himself as a kind of 'schnorrer,'
that is, a beggar with his hand out, and this isn't an

image that the Israeli likes to accept of himself. The Israeli image is more of a hard-muscled parachutist or pirate! But we are still dependent on the U.S. . . . in fact our adverse balance of payments is made up by money from the U.S."

"Americans are disliked by Israelis," said the grown son of an American kibbutznik. "American tourists are horrible in the whole world, and also in Israel, and especially the Jews. American Jews gave money to help build Israel and they feel they have some ownership in it. An American tourist will walk around the kibbutz and look in wherever he wants. If anybody says anything to him, he'll be hurt. He thinks about it as his place and everything in it as his. They walk around that way, especially elderly people who gave any money. When the youth groups come here, they are looked on not as Jews but as Americans, and they are forced to carry the American flag. Israelis make them answer for everything from American policy to the American tourist, and they find themselves fighting the fight of the Americans and feeling more American than they do in America."

During an evening spent with some American students in Jerusalem I listened to much vehement talk, both offensive and defensive, along these lines. There was a certain embarrassed contempt expressed for "American" money values, and much was said about the practice of putting donors' names on plaques, as though this were a peculiarly Jewish or American-

Jewish habit. On the other hand, as one young man sagely observed, Israel wants and needs the money it gets from America, and Israelis would dearly love to have all the things that American money can buy. "All I can see," he said, "is that Israelis want TV, they want cars, they want vacations, they want money they can travel with. Israeli students go to the U.S. and don't come back in droves. And it's no joke here about Israeli girls 'marrying for passports' "—there was laughter at this, apparently at the expense of certain young people in the room who were in the midst of romances—"they all want either to go to the U.S. or else to have what people in the U.S. have. So it's really a combination of admiration and resentment all mixed up."

Americans who have settled in Israel are also looked on as "rich Americans" by the Israeli bureaucracy, which concludes therefrom that Americans need no help, and by Israelis generally, who envy them for it. Americans *are* often materially better off than a great many people in Israel and they feel this difference with a certain embarrassment. On the other hand, a great many Americans living in Israel feel anything but "rich"—they feel pinched and poor and pressed to struggle hard to maintain what most of them feel is a lower standard of living than they like. This complicates their embarrassment at being viewed by Israelis as "rich Americans"; it makes them feel uncomfortable about themselves, and this comes out in the form of resentment against Israelis who, they know, would dearly love to be "rich" too.

Deeper American Imprints

But there are much more meaningful, much deeper-cutting ways in which his *American* identity has imposed itself on the experience of the American Jew in Israel. An American visitor to Israel nearly fifteen years ago noted that American Zionists who had gone to settle there were less steeped in ideology than their European comrades, and that whether they knew it consciously or not, had been largely fashioned by the pragmatism of James and the instrumentalism of Dewey, and that this gave them a less "holy" view of Zionist tradition and a much greater readiness to submit experience to "trial and error." He noted as an example that Americans who had come to Israel to join the highly doctrinaire kibbutz movement very soon began to resist some of its ideas about child rearing. They wanted mothers to "spend more time with their children" while Europeans shrugged: "Why indulge the children the way all Americans do?* It was at a predominantly American kibbutz, just a few years ago, that the issue was fought to a decision which took infant children out of the communal children's houses and put them back home with their mothers, much to

* Ira Eisenstein, "Americans in Israel," *The Reconstructionist,* January 26, 1951.

the horror of the more rigid European communalists and some of their American emulators. Greatly liberalized styles of child rearing have been adopted, I was told in 1963, at eleven kibbutzim, the majority with heavy American or "Anglo-Saxon" membership. At one large kibbutz where the battle over keeping young children at home was lost by four votes, the high emotions generated by the struggle still hung in the air. In my own very fragmentary encounters with parents and children in these settings, I got the impression of family experience that was still very different indeed from that of the American family in America, but also very different from that of European families in the same kibbutzim. A key notion that kept flickering through some of these conversations: the children of American parents thought they were a good deal more at ease—"freer" was the word—at home with their parents than European children were.

Americans bring a distinctive experience of their own also to what is perhaps the most critical of all the situations faced internally by the new Jewish state— the problem that has come to be called "the two Israels." This is the problem of acculturation, integration, and assimilation raised by the coming together in Israel of two major streams of European and non-European Jews, the latter now comprising more than half of the Israeli population. This has moved to the center of Israeli concerns, scarcely second even to the overriding care for security from Arab attack. The way it is resolved will determine the future shape of the new Israeli society. It will determine not only the cultural but also the physical characteristics of the "Israeli" who will emerge from it. For here, under the over-arching mantle of a still largely undefined common "Jewishness" in a tiny land facing all the tasks of rapid development within and hostile foes without, a confrontation takes place between Ashkenazi and Sephardi Jews that turns out also to be an encounter between European and non-European, "Western" and "Eastern," "modern" and "traditional," industrialized and nonindustrialized, skilled and nonskilled, educated and uneducated—and also "white" and "non-white." As anyone can see who stands on a street anywhere in Israel, the ingathering of the wandering tribes has shown dramatically to what extent Jews have become not only the cultural but also the physical products of the cultures in which they lived as "outsiders" for so long. European Jews appear in all the ethnic varieties of Europeans, and "Oriental" Jews appear in all the shades of "whiteness" to "semi-whiteness" to "non-whiteness" of skin common among the various peoples of the countries in which they lived. Jews seeking to regain homogeneity in Israel now have to bridge not only all the great differences of culture and civilization that separate peoples of industrialized and nonindustrialized societies, but they also have to close the gap of color.

This produces in Israel a peculiarly "American" condition. It reproduces in its own forms in the Israeli society many of the same problems of integration and assimilation that have been unfolding in the American society. In the United States, government, institutions, and people have been struggling against recalcitrant or intractable social, economic, and psychological facts of life in order to achieve the greater integration that the society now needs and demands. Israel now confronts a situation that contains many of these same elements. All kinds of Israeli Jews are trying to make their way through this sea of troubles, but American Jews come upon it along a course all their own. Unlike any other Jews who have come to Israel, they come from a society whose motto is *E pluribus unum* and whose national credo calls for a common equality of rights shared by all together with a mutual respect for differences among groups and kinds of people. Jews in America have had a large part in the continuing struggle to translate this American credo into American reality. For Jews this has in recent decades been more and more successfully realized, and in recent years at an irregularly accelerating pace Negroes have been moving with them out onto that great open common center of American life where all Americans, regardless of race, creed, or color, are entitled to enjoy their full equality of rights. The American Jews who come to Israel come from a country that—with all its difficulties—is in the process of becoming more free, more open, more effectively plural every year. No other people from any of the many countries from which Jews have come to Israel can make that statement. It is in many ways the most unique American uniqueness there is.

How this is reflected in the experience and behavior of American Jews in Israel is something that flickered in and out of my own interviews there. Partly it was wrapped up in those complex reasons for migration which we have already explored, but even most of those who described themselves as feeling most excluded as "Jews" in America tended to insist on the strength of their continued attachment to the political and social ideas they had absorbed as "Americans" and in their wish to re-create them on Israeli soil. At the same time, of course, they reflected all the varieties one would expect to find in any cross section of people. On the score of how they related to the special problem of group separateness in Israel, they showed up with everything from heightened sensitivity to the cruder forms of prejudice. But my own soundings on this matter were too few to yield up any sense of any larger common pattern among them and this must remain, like so much else in this exploratory inquiry, a subject for further scrutiny. But this much at least was clear: American Jews seeking some greater "Jewish" homogeneity in Israel find themselves instead meeting a far greater heterogeneity among Jews than most of them had ever thought to find. It makes the key problems of the Israeli society look a lot like the problems of the

American society they left behind, and solving them is going to call for the adaptation of what might be called *American* solutions. What part Americans in Israel will play in this process will depend on what parts they find it possible to play in helping to shape the Israel to which they want to belong.

Sholom Kahn, who now teaches American literature at Hebrew University, wrote in 1955 of "The Pangs of Aliyah"* and touched upon "those aspects of life in Israel which may trouble [an American Jew's] Americanism." He began his list with the problem of the lower standard of living, and then went on to speak of the rigidities of Israeli political and trade union life. He thought that the Zionist brand of socialism on the one hand created an "unjust inequality"—especially as it affected the status of teachers—while on the other hand leaving room for powerfully acquisitive practices and "exorbitant profits" in certain other economic sectors. Americans appreciate competition, he wrote, "but they resent being taken for 'suckers,' and they have been trained by their history to be suspicious of 'robber barons' who use the slogans of national idealism." Kahn wrote too of something he called, searching

* Sholom J. Kahn, "The Pangs of Aliyah," *The Reconstructionist*, January 21, 1955. See also Sholom J. Kahn, "Israel's First Pentad," *The Menorah Journal*, Summer, 1954. A brief but extremely perceptive examination of the subject will be found in Ernest Stock, "Americans in Israel," *Midstream*, Summer, 1957.

for a better word, *provincialism*—"I am referring to an almost physical sensation of smallness and narrowness which is likely to strike the American, accustomed to more spacious horizons." But he wrote most feelingly of all on the subject of religion. Kahn who, unlike many European Zionists but like a great many other American Jews in Israel, is religious in his own way, found himself deeply troubled by the shape of the problem of Judaism in Jewish Israel. He quoted a visiting American rabbi as saying—something I heard said more than once during my brief travels in Israel—that "there is a brighter future for 'Judaism'—as distinct from mere 'Jewishness'—in America than in Israel." Kahn concluded with a certain sad dismay that it "is no more easy to be a Jew in Israel than it is in America."

7. Being "Jews"

The difficulty about being a "Jew" is that nobody can say who or what a "Jew" is and nobody agrees with anybody else on what the "Jewish life" is. These are old questions to which many different answers have been made over a rather long period of time, whether by the "Jew" of the Bible, the "Jew" created in the ghettos of the dispersion, the "Jew" defined at Nuremburg, or the "Jew"—Reform, Conservative, Orthodox —variously self-labeled by individual choice among Jews in America during the last few generations. For most of this time, just as Negroes could be described in the words of the late Kelly Miller, as "anybody who'd be jimcrowed in Virginia," Jews could be described as anybody taken by the Gentile world to be a Jew, or as anybody who regarded himself as a Jew. Whatever the complications, these definitions served for most practical purposes for a long time. But now these old questions press hard in a new way for new answers. For now there is a Jewish State of Israel, where a leader like David Ben-Gurion quotes the

Talmud to say—to the dismayed outrage of most Jews in America—that a Jew outside Israel now is a Jew "without God," i.e., really not a true Jew at all. Ben-Gurion was not actually charging the great mass of American Jews with godlessness, but twitting Orthodox literalists for their inconsistency. On the other hand, the State of Israel supports an official religious establishment which claims—often to the dismayed outrage of many of Israel's secular leaders—that it alone can say who and what a Jew rightly is. Since the Israeli rabbinate officially holds power over the personal status of all Jews in Israel, governing all matters having to do with marriage, divorce, birth, and legitimacy, it uses it to decide by its own interpretations of Jewish religious law who is validly a "Jew" and what is validly "Jewish." This becomes much more than a broad legal, philosophic, or religious matter. It assumes intensely personal forms, such as whether one is married or living in sin, or whether one's children are bastards or not. As one American in Jerusalem wryly put it: "Where else in the world could I live where no one knows who's a Jew, what's a Zionist, or who's married?" These issues are forced to the point of decision in actual case after case. Each of these decisions most directly affects Jews in Israel, but also forces Jews outside Israel—who are of course not legally subject to any decision made in Israel—to decide whether and how far they share whatever seems to be becoming the official Israeli view of their Jewish identity.

Defining a "Jew" in Israel has become an issue in politics, among other things. In 1958 the question split one of David Ben-Gurion's coalition cabinets when there was a contest between the secular and religious authorities over how the identification "Jew" could be claimed by Jews in Israel, whether, as Ben-Gurion's Minister of Interior insisted, by a simple personal affirmation, or as the Religious authorities demanded, by proof that a person was truly a Jew as defined by Jewish religious law, i.e., the child of a Jewish mother. The issue was debated for months in Parliament and in the press and Ben-Gurion appealed to Jewish rabbinical and lay leaders to come up with an acceptable definition of "Jew," but it was all to no avail; the confusion only grew deeper.

The business of defining a "Jew" in Israel has become very largely a business of court fights and court decisions, and great tugs of war between the secular Israeli authority, represented in these matters by the dominant government parties and the Supreme Court of Israel on the one hand, and the Religious establishment on the other, represented by the officially supported rabbinate with its own councils and rabbinical courts on the ecclesiastical side, and the Religious parties in politics, with a Minister of Religion drawn from their ranks sitting in the cabinet,* always in these

* The elements of present relations between the state and religion in Israel come partly out of the history of Zionism and partly out of the history of Palestine. Nonreligious or antireligious secular Zionism was countered by the creation of a number of religiously oriented parties within the movement. Political parties were also formed by older ultra-

years as a member of a fragile coalition. Some of the
most celebrated of these hotly contested decisions have
been widely reported and discussed. One of the most
notable was the decision in 1962 in the case of Brother
Daniel, a Polish Jew who became a Carmelite monk
and who on coming to Israel claimed Israeli citizenship
as a Jew coming in under the Law of Return. The Law
had failed to define what a "Jew" was—perhaps because its makers in 1950 did not know or did not
dream it would become an issue, for who would want
to declare himself a Jew if he wasn't a Jew?—and
Brother Daniel presented the court with a remarkably
scrambled set of possible definitions. There are apparently not a few apostate Jews in Israel as members of
various Christian religious orders—in his *Wild Goats
of Ein Gedi* Herbert Weiner reports a number of
encounters with such individuals—but Brother Daniel

---

religious groups in Palestine outside of Zionism. Three such Religious
parties function as a bloc in Israel politics now and represent the political
arm of the Orthodox establishment. The rabbinical council and courts,
however, were established in Palestine during the Turkish Empire and
continued during the period of the British Mandate, under a system
whereby each religious group maintained its own structure and ad-
ministered its own laws relating to matters of personal status for its own
constituencies, and also represented its group in dealings with the governing authority. The new State of Israel guaranteed "freedom of religion,
conscience, language, education, and culture" to all religious groups.
Authority over Jews as a religious group, however, passed to the Orthodox
rabbinical establishment. In return for their support in a coalition which
enabled the social-democratic Mapai to govern without the more radical
Soviet-oriented Mapam, the Religious parties exacted greater and greater
concessions of authority to the rabbinical council. For a brief summary
and outline of this background, see Joseph Badi, *Religion in Israel Today*,
New York, 1959. Cf. also Ronald Sanders, *Israel, The View from Masada*,
New York, 1966, pp. 286–299.

was an unusually sympathetic figure who had made a
heroic record helping Jews in Nazi Poland. As the son
of a Jewish mother, he was a "Jew" by religious law,
but the Court ruled that this definition was not the
only one to be taken into consideration. Although its
members split along various lines on the issue, the
decision was that while there could be nonreligious or
even atheistic Jews, there could be no such thing as a
Catholic Jew. Brother Daniel was found to be not a
"Jew," not because he had forsaken the Jewish religion
but because he had embraced another; apostasy cut the
tie. He was entitled to become an Israeli by naturaliza-
tion but not by natural rights which he had forfeited
by leaving the community of Jews. Just what a "Jew"
really was, the Court avoided saying, leaving the
matter to something it called "the common understanding," even though it was clear that not all could
agree on what that "common understanding" might be
at any given moment or might become in the future.*

* For an exposition of the Brother Daniel case see Marc Galanter, "A
Dissent on Brother Daniel," *Commentary*, July, 1963. For a reference to
another celebrated case in which the "common understanding" became
the basis for a decision of a matter of identity—in this instance a decision
by the United States Supreme Court on a Hindu's claim that he was
"white"—see Isaacs, *Scratches on Our Minds, American Images of China
and India*, New York, 1958, pp. 284, 290. Another case that attracted
attention in Israel during 1965 involved some curious twists on the official
definitions of "religion" and "nationality." This was the case of Ilana
Stern, a Russian-born eighteen-year-old girl, daughter of a Jewish father
and a mother whose religious affiliation was "unknown." Because of this
the Ministry of Interior registered her as "Christian" by religion and said
her "nationality" was "under consideration." She sued in the high court
to force the Ministry to register her as a "Jew" by nationality and to erase
the designation "Christian" since she declared herself to be an atheist.

Another case that more recently stirred all Israel is that of Mrs. Rita Eitani, wife of a German Jew, a heroine of the flight from Nazi Germany, the illegal immigration, the struggle against the British, and the war against the Arabs. Mrs. Eitani became a municipal official in the city of Nazareth, where she clashed with Religious authorities on a whole series of issues. They picked up a rumor that she was the daughter of a non-Jewish mother and actually sent to Germany for confirmation from available Nazi "racial" records. With this proof in hand, they proceeded to challenge the legality of her Israeli citizenship—which she had acquired automatically as a "Jew" under the Law of Return—and both the validity of her marriage and the legitimacy of her children. In December, 1964, the Interior Ministry refused to renew Mrs. Eitani's passport on the grounds that she was not a citizen, since she was not a "Jew" and therefore not entitled to citizenship under the Law of Return. Mrs. Eitani could only become a "Jew" in Israel by going through a ritual conversion, which she finally did in the fall of 1966.* She could presumably regain her Israeli citizenship by getting naturalized and legitimize her marriage and

---

She won her case, finally getting a card on which she was declared to be of "Jewish" nationality. This proved, her attorney said, "the absurdity of their official stand that Jewish nationality and religion are inseparable." The young woman's identity card now notes that her mother's religion was "unclear." Thus while she is now "Jewish" by civil definition, she is not "Jewish" as far as the Religious authorities are concerned. "This means," the lawyer went on, "that Miss Stern is now the only Jewish 'national' in this country who cannot be married here."—*Jerusalem Post*, August 20 and October 22, 1965.

* *Jerusalem Post*, September 23, 1966.

her children, in the eyes of the Religious authorities, only by going through their prescribed ceremony. As this case made its way through the maze of religious and secular justice in Israel, it became the center of deeply troubled controversy among people of all persuasions in the country.* It was clearly not going to be possible for believers in modern political and social democracy—among all kinds of Israelis but least of all for Americans—or for seekers after some new religious definition within Judaism, to continue accepting the dominance of this kind of clericalism without suffering mortal corrosion in the process.

Court decisions in Israel cannot answer the key questions. Is a Jew someone who believes in Judaism? Is he the product or heir of Jewish history? Is the "Jewish life" a national life, a religious life, or this or that version or combination of either or both? Are Jews a "nation," a "people," a "folk," an assembly of believers in a certain creed? And if the latter, what creed, as defined when, by whom, and how practiced, and fitting where in the modern world? The questions are old questions, but they have newly become the urgent issues of rediscovery and redefinition. To pursue them is to move quickly into much deeper parts of this maze, crowded with confusion and hot with controversy and high emotion. For this is the group identity crisis into which Jews have been pushed by the

* Cf. J. L. Talmon, "Who is a Jew?," *Encounter,* May, 1965.

great events that have so profoundly affected them all in this generation: the Hitlerian holocaust, the creation of the State of Israel, and the rapid opening of the open society in the United States. Under these impacts everything about the Jewish identity has come up for scrutiny and change. The discussion already fills a vast literature and its sounds can be heard wherever Jews come together in their numerous groups in conferences, dialogues, debates, or just plain conversation. Whether in Israel, in America, or elsewhere, Jews are trying to discover anew what it means to be Jews, what the Jewish religion is, what "Jewishness" is, what Israel means for the future of Jews, Judaism, and Jewishness, whether in Israel or outside of it, what Jews should do or what they should not do to save, preserve, or promote what this or that group thinks should be saved, preserved, or promoted. These are all formidably arguable matters, and I do not propose to join in the argument here. But from it all at least one thing emerges clearly: it no longer suffices, as it did for so long, to define the Jewish identity in terms of Jewish outsiderness. The great bulk of the world's Jews are moving "inside" now—two million of them "inside" Jewish Israel and nearly six million more and more "inside" pluralist America. In both these new locations, Jews are being forced to define in some new and more positive way what they are. And from this at least one more thing follows: from these two very differently situated clusters of Jews facing these questions quite different answers will come. In deciding who and what

they are, they will produce quite different rearrange-
ments of all the elements of their group identity: their
view of their history and origins, their religion, nationality, language, even their color and physical characteristics—the whole mix of culture-past and culture-
present out of which group identity is made.

These matters press hard on all Jews, on Jews in
Israel and on Jews in America between whom complicated differences have appeared over some of the most
basic issues of religion and nationality and the meaning of the "Jewish life." For this reason it presses
perhaps with more particular sharpness on the small
number of American Jews who are trying either to
bridge these differences or to choose between them by
attempting to live their lives in Israel. They are having
a complicated experience and perhaps one day one of
them will write an account that will better illuminate
some of its many parts. From my own brief inquiry,
meanwhile, I can only suggest some of the things that
came into view as I put my questions, got my answers,
and tried to discover what some of these answers might
mean.

Sartre's "Jews"

Here, to begin with, we again meet some of those
Jews who had "solved the Jewish question" by coming
to Israel. As long used by Zionists, the phrase "the
Jewish Question" had to do not with what it meant to
be a Jew, but with what it meant to be a "Jew" among

Gentiles. It had to do with the minority status of Jews among hostile Gentile majorities. It had to do with anti-Semitism. The "Jewish" question in this context was in substance the "Gentile" question. Solving it meant getting out from under the Gentiles, escaping from this "minorityness" to a "majorityness" in at least one place Jews could again hold as their own. For some individuals who used this phrase, it seemed to be quite enough in itself to get away from the Gentiles, from that presence in which one felt uneasy or afraid, or even at best, as one American in Israel suggested in his own case, to get away from the intolerable sense of being a tolerated guest in someone else's house. One came to Israel, then, not so much to *be* a Jew but to *cease being* the "Jew" as seen by the anti-Semitic majority Gentiles from whom one was fleeing. Hence the plain relief of those solvers of "the Jewish question" who said they were happy in Israel because in Israel, "you can forget about being a Jew, it's no problem."

This was a fairly common remark among American Jews one met in Israel, but in those who also spoke of being "authentic Jews" or "non-authentic Jews," it was easy to recognize readers of Jean-Paul Sartre's 1946 essay on anti-Semitism. It proved to be an instructive experience to look back to Sartre's pages for the "Jew" in whom they had recognized themselves.*

* All quotations from Sartre, *Anti-Semite and Jew*, Grove Press Black Cat Paperback edition, New York, 1962.

For Sartre, Jews are "nothing" in themselves but are creatures who exist only in "the hostility and disdain of the societies which surround them." Deprived by the Christian society of his history, his national or religious identity, the Jew becomes a person with "a phantom personality, at once strange and familiar, that haunts him, and which is nothing but himself as others see him." For Sartre, "it is neither their past, their religion, nor their soil that unites the sons of Israel. If they have a common bond . . . it is because they have in common the situation of Jew" and this situation is to be the object of hate and rejection. "We must ask," says Sartre, "not 'What is a Jew' but 'What have you made of the Jews?' " Sartre's "non-authentic Jews" are those who "deal with their situation by running away from it." This "does not necessarily mean that they wish to destroy the concept of the Jew or that they explicitly deny the existence of a Jewish reality. But their gestures, sentiments, and acts aim secretly at destroying this reality." The non-authentic Jew "sets out to prove in his own person that there are no Jews" and his "anxiety" comes out of his "fear of acting and feeling like a Jew."

Sartre's "authentic Jew," on the other hand, undertakes "to live to the full his condition as a Jew." This requires, Sartre goes on, that "he knows himself and wills himself into history as a historic and damned creature; he ceases to run away from himself and to be ashamed of his own kind. . . . He knows that he is

one who stands apart, untouchable, scorned, pro-
scribed—and it is *as such* [Sartre's italics] that he
asserts his being. . . . He chooses his brothers and his
peers; they are the other Jews. He stakes everything on
human grandeur, for he accepts the obligation to live
in a situation that is defined precisely by the fact that it
is unlivable; he derives his pride from his humiliation." Sartre's "authentic Jew" has the option of trying
to be authentic in this fashion wherever he happens to
be, or "he may also persuade himself that Jewish
authenticity demands that the Jew be sustained by a
Jewish national community." But while this will give
"certainty to the Jew on the ethical level," it will "in
no way serve as a solution on the social or political
level: the situation of the Jew is such that everything
he does turns against him."

Describing the "non-authentic Jews" who run away
from their situation, Sartre says:

> When therefore they are by themselves in the inti-
> macy of their apartments, by eliminating the non-Jewish
> witness, they eliminate Jewish reality at the same time.
> No doubt those Christians who have penetrated these
> interiors find their inhabitants more Jewish than ever
> but that is because they have allowed themselves to re-
> lax—which does not mean that they abandon themselves
> to the enjoyment of their Jewish "nature," as they are
> often accused of doing, but on the contrary that they
> forget it.

Now the Sartrian disciple one encounters among
American Jews in Israel is one who believes that by

choosing to come to Israel he has asserted his Sartrian authenticity, accepting his "condition" as a Jew. But if, as Sartre suggests, Jewish authenticity consists of stoically accepting a "condition" of untouchable, un-livable humiliation, it should be no surprise that once these Jews come authentically to Israel, they proceed, in the privacy of their all-Jewish community out of sight of that Gentile witness, not to "abandon them-selves to the enjoyment of their Jewish nature," but, like Sartre's non-authentics, do their best to "forget" that they are Jews. In Israel, they say, therefore, ex-plaining why they are happy there, "you can forget about being a Jew—it's no problem."

"Jew" and "Israeli"

Sartre's genteel, Gentile-aping, assimilating "Jew" is not the only Diaspora Jew who comes up now on charges of non-authenticity. Some Zionists in Israel make the same charge against that other more heavily sterotyped Diaspora Jew, the non-genteel, Gentile-avoiding Eastern European ghetto Jew. Indeed, at the Zionist bar, all Diaspora Jews stand indicted on this charge. This has to do with the Zionist view of Jewish history, a highly controversial matter among Jews for a long time.

It is the strongly held view of an influential segment of Israel's Zionist elite that the last prideful chapter of Jewish history ended when the last Israeli resistance to the invaders collapsed in Jerusalem in the year 70, or

with Bar Kochba's revolt in the year 132, and that the
Diaspora that followed was a long dark age in which
the Jew became a creature of weakness and of shame.
According to this view of things, proper Jewish history
was resumed only in 1948 when hard-muscled, hard-
fighting Jews re-established the State of Israel and
made it possible at last for all Jews to become Israelis
again. This "leap in time" to the glories of the remote
Jewish past is one that all young people in Israel are
urged to make. Their identifications as Jews go back to
the heroes and the people of the Bible. This carries
with it on its underside a strongly negative view of
Diaspora Jewry, and above all of the Eastern European
Jewry from which this Zionist elite stems and from
which its younger Israel-born members are barely a
generation removed.

In the flow of these attitudes and feelings about the
past, different pools of meaning have begun to form
around the terms "Jew" and "Israeli." One comes
upon them readily enough in Israel now, among both
the old and the young of this tradition, but especially
among the young. To be an "Israeli" means not to be
the "Jew" whom the Gentile world held in contempt
for so long, and this is essentially the Jew represented
by the whole stock of anti-Semitic stereotypes built up
around the Diaspora Jew, or more specifically around
the East European Jew. Being in Zion means to be no
longer a pale and puny and money-trading "Jew," but
a tanned and muscular and strong soil-tilling "Israeli,"

no longer cringing and defenseless, no longer a home-
less Yiddish-speaking wanderer unwanted and scorned
everywhere, but a Hebrew-speaking citizen of one's
own ancient land, reclaimed by the strength of one's
own arms and prowess and stoutly held by the same
means. In its various shadings and degrees of feeling,
this view of the Diaspora Jew remains an integral part
of the new Israeli self-image created by cutting across
2,000 years of history, trying to drop as much as possible of the design woven during all this time and to pick
up instead the threads of that more glorious past of
long, long ago.

There are of course many different shapes in which
this Israeli image of the "Jew" appears. It varies in
coloring and sharpness from group to group and especially, like everything else in Israel, from the older to
the younger generation. Like everything else also in
Israel now, it generates conflicting emotions, controversy, and a kind of suspended confusion that comes
out of a common unwillingness to force such issues, to
allow them, rather, to work themselves out in time.
This rejection of the Diaspora past has taken forms of
self-rejection strong enough and crude enough to be
seen as a form of Zionist anti-Semitism. It has been
strong enough to lead to a countereffort, through the
introduction of a course called "Jewish Consciousness"
in Israeli schools, to redress the balance in the minds of
young people between the Biblical and the Diaspora
periods of the Jewish past.

Some of these issues have been folded into the remarkable revival of Hebrew as the language of Israel, for this involved a whole set of attitudes toward *Yiddishkeit,* the East European culture that was built around the use of the Yiddish language. There are still many Yiddish-speaking Jews in Hebrew-speaking Israel, but the use of Yiddish was sharply discouraged by Zionists who saw it as an obstacle to the revival of Hebrew as well as a symbol of the mongrelization of the Jews in the Diaspora. The parting and the joining of the Yiddish and Hebrew strands in the new culture of Israel is, again, in some part a matter of generation: the constituency for Yiddish literature and the Yiddish theater is among the older and more recent immigrants, not among the Israeli-born youth. There is a Yiddish-language paper now in Israel with a circulation, I was told, of 25,000—larger than that of the English-language *Jerusalem Post*—and in the last few years there has been a reappearance of Yiddish theater, marked by the 1965 success of a play based on the work of a contemporary Yiddish poet, Itzik Manger. The show played to empty seats until "Yiddish theatregoers, mostly elderly immigrants from Rumania," according to a newspaper report, began to come to the out-of-the-way theater where it was playing. The musical *Fiddler on the Roof,* created in English in New York out of Sholem Aleichem's famous stories of Eastern European ghetto life, was produced in Israel in a Hebrew version. The leading role of Tevye was played by a Sabra—an Israeli-born—actor, who was criticized as lacking "the

Jewish touch." The Hebrew script of the play was described as "a banal travesty of Sholem Aleichem." The Tevye of the play told an interviewer that "as far as he was concerned, the fact that Tevye was a Jew was coincidental. He said he portrayed the situation, not the Jew." When the Sabra player was replaced by a sixty-year-old actor born in the Ukraine, the whole production was transformed, according to this account by an American reporter, because "the new Tevye . . . is as authentically Jewish as tsimmis"—tsimmis being a candied-carrot dish favored by Russian Jews and still familiar at least to second-generation Jewish Americans.*

Whatever the surviving or reviving ambivalence among Israelis toward European Yiddishkeit, there seemed to be much less question about its American cousin, contemptuously referred to by some American Jews as "borscht-circuit Yiddishkeit." A veteran American settler in Jerusalem told me: "The Yiddishkeit of American Jews is foreign to Israel. Why, Danny Kaye came here and thought he had it in the bag among all these Jews, but he just fell flat. They sat on their hands at his patter until he began to sing a non-Jewish song of some kind. The same goes for the joke about Ben-Gurion in the Vaughn Meader record about the Kennedys. It just doesn't go here. Israelis read Sholem Aleichem in school in Hebrew translation. They eat blintzes and kugel, not bagels and lox."

* *New York Times,* January 23, 1966.

The image of the Diaspora Jew apparently gets some of its harshest treatment in the conflict between the most militant antireligious and ultrareligious groups. "I saw a demonstration here," said a recently arrived American, "in which some labor movement group was marching in protest about some action by the Religious Party, and they carried a huge cartoon figure of one of the religious types—in caftan and with earlocks and so on—which had a face that might just as well have appeared in *Der Sturmer* in Hitler Germany." This was, I was assured, an extremism most Israelis did not share. I found the same caricature oddly reproduced in wood carvings sold to tourists in shops and it appeared again, albeit in a much more good-natured setting, in the costuming, makeup, and gestures used by a young Israeli dance troupe I saw entertaining at a tourist hotel when, among their proudly rendered folk dances, they also gave their version of a Hasidic wedding dance in a manner that seemed calculated to win—and did win—uncomfortably derisive laughter from an audience made up largely of visiting Americans. Here again, I was assured by embarrassed Israelis that this attitude of mockery was "not typical." Some years ago Professor Simon Herman of Hebrew University reported on American students in Israel who found Sabras "less Jewish than they wished or expected them to be," and who found problems in "the difference between Jewishness and Israeliness.* During my

* Simon Herman, "American Jewish Students in Israel," *Jewish Social Studies*, XXIV: 1, January, 1962, p. 13.

own visit to Jerusalem I heard an American student report on one of his own experiments in a mixed Israeli-American class with lists of paired qualities to be attributed to "Israelis" or "Jews." He reported with some indignant dismay that the Israeli students in the class tended to assign the most favorable qualities in a lopsided way to the "Israeli" (who was seen as clean, progressive, a man of action, tall, aggressive, self-respecting, self-confident, strong, free) and to ascribe a much greater share of the opposite negative attributes to "Jew" (dirty, regressive, man of words, short, defensive, lacking self-respect, lacking in self-confidence, weak, constrained). The American students were much more ambivalent, since they generally also admired the Israelis, but did not see either themselves or their friends or parents in the guise of the standard stereotyped ghetto Jew.

I cannot report in any systematic way on the distribution or currency of these prejudices. But they are clearly not uncommon, especially among young people. At an American-Israeli "Dialogue" in mid-1963, an American resident of Israel said:

> "When I first came to Israel, I had a discussion with an Israeli girl. She firmly denied being Jewish and identified herself as an 'Israeli.' She said: 'What have I in common with some Jew in Paris who has a long beard and stinks from garlic?' That kind of remark we often hear from . . . young Israeli Jews; and only yesterday one of them admitted to me that they are the worst anti-Semites around. . . . I have found . . . gross failure

on the part of Israeli youth . . . to hold up their heads as Jews."*

Many individuals referred to these attitudes in my own conversations and interviews in Israel, and many seemed troubled by them. When a young man, the Sabra son of a veteran American settler, brashly voiced the not uncommon view that Hitler's victims were "cowards," his father winced and reached for some softer word. Perhaps the strongest expression of feeling reflecting this view of the "Jew" turned up at the end of a long and wide-ranging conversation I had with a young man who had come to Israel from a Zionist youth group in New York, spent several years on a kibbutz, and then became a city dweller pursuing his own professional interests. We had been talking about Israel's future. "Well, we may get it here," he said, somewhat ruminatively, "who knows, we are sur-rounded by seventy million Arabs, and in five years or ten or twenty—" He shrugged. "But if they come in," he went on, his voice rising, "they'll have to come in fighting, and if we have to die we'll die"—I thought he was going to say die *fighting,* or die as *men,* but instead he finished—"if we have to die, we'll die as Zionists and Israelis, *not as Jews!*" He spat out the unexpected word *Jews* with a savage passion that pinned me back in my seat.

This was, to be sure, again an extreme example, but

* "Second Dialogue in Israel," *Congress Bi-Weekly,* 30:12, September 16, 1963, p. 39.

it did show what could happen when you asked an American Jew in Israel what it meant to be a *Jew*. More commonly the answers were much lower-keyed, and much more often led straight to the subject of religion. This took us swiftly into the deepest heart of the maze, for of all that goes to make up the Jewish identity, nothing is more central, more fundamental, and more confused than the matter of the Jewish religion and its place in the whole process of rediscovery and redefinition now going on. A young man on a kibbutz in the north, son of an American settler, said:

"Being a Jew means to me a moral code that I live by. This has nothing to do with God, but is a basic way of thought, the rich cultural background, the Bible through all the years. . . ."

And on the same kibbutz an older American said:

"All of us are Jews by birth, desire, profession, but in my opinion the definition of being a Jew has to include some kind of affinity to God."

"Religious" Jews and "Nonreligious" Jews

A would-be American settler who had been in Israel for about a year spoke ruefully about an Israeli friend of his who had migrated in the opposite direction, from Israel to America, and had written to him: "Zion is *here*. The true Jewish life is in Chicago and New York, not in Israel at all." The "Jewish life" in this case meant the religious life, which the Israeli was finding it easier to lead according to his own lights in America than the American was finding it in Israel.

The phrase "the two Israels" usually refers to the presence of the two main segments of the present Israeli population, the European and the non-European. Hardly any less portentous or less critical for Israel's future as a Jewish state is that other division among Israel's Jews, roughly between the "religious" and the "nonreligious" or, in some cases, the "anti-religious." These lines sometimes intersect. The issue of religion in Israel is wrapped up in the issue of the nature of Jewish culture and the way it has to be reshaped in a modern Israel. Along with integration of peoples and cultures, Israel also has to bring about, if it can, some new religious synthesis that will be meaningfully accepted by the people of a Jewish state. Both of these processes are most hopefully seen as taking place only over several generations, producing in time not only a new modern Jew but new modern Jewish answers to the old questions about how Jews confront the human condition, and how they understand man's relationship to God. On this score there has been some beginning of searching debate and discussion.* But in its present actual condition, the religious division in Israel also forces critical issues at much closer range. They rise sharply and unpostponably in the everyday affairs of the country and of each person in it. Indeed,

* E.g., cf. Ernst Simon, "Are We Israelis Still Jews?" *Commentary*, April, 1953.

if it were not for the constant Arab threat, an Israeli scholar told an inquiring American Reform rabbi, these tensions "would make us explode from within. In a way the Arab wall of hostility is our salvation, for at least this period of our history. This is not quite the time to be setting off religious explosions here."* But friction on this issue is almost constant. It heats up over matters that often go right to the center of the deepest problems of the new state and the new society coming into being there. Those who count on future generations to provide the answers are often trying not to notice how the present generation is determining the shape of the questions that will have to be answered. The perplexity, however, is great and confounding. Professor J. L. Talmon, Hebrew University's noted historian, in a recent article under the perennially recurring title "Who Is a Jew?"** wrote: "It would be difficult to imagine a more complex, more insoluble, indeed a more poignant problem than the question of religion and state in present-day Israel." At the end of a detailed review of religious affairs in the country, he somberly concluded: "The Jewish religion may paradoxically be facing its supreme test precisely in the Jewish state, and the problem of Jewish identity may prove even more in-

* Herbert Weiner, *The Wild Goats of Ein Gedi,* New York, 1963. Rabbi Weiner's book reports on extended exploration of the state of religion in Israel. Its nonpolemical character is rare in the small literature that exists on this big subject.
** "A Letter From Israel," *Encounter,* May, 1965.

tractable in the Jewish National Home than in the countries of dispersion."

One of the most common phrases used by Americans in Israel to explain the Israeli religious situation to a visitor is: "Here you are either *Orthodox* or you are *nothing*."

Only some small number of American Jews in Israel, I think it is fair to guess, are "Orthodox," or "religious" in the Israeli meaning of that term. Being "religious" in Israel means observing the Jewish religious practice prescribed and supervised by the official rabbinical establishment. This official Orthodoxy is flanked on its right by ultra-Orthodox groups some of which, like the Naturei Karta, refuse to recognize the State of Israel, seeing it as a man-created fraud anticipating the true coming of the Messiah. But the official Orthodoxy itself goes far beyond the American-style Orthodoxy in which many, if not most, of Israel's American Jewish settlers were raised. In Israel the word used is not "Orthodox" but "pious" or "observant" and this is made synonymous with "religious." This is often rendered as "Religious"—the capital letter signifying the official place of the ecclesiastical authorities in the country's affairs, with rabbis and schools supported by government funds, members of Religious parties sitting in the Parliament, and the Minister of Religion in the cabinet. This establishment is supported by American Orthodox groups of various kinds, such as the Mizrachi organization, and there are some Americans in Israel who live and work in this milieu with the support of their parent organizations.

Some larger—but still small—number of American Jews in Israel probably are "nothing," which in Israel means that they share some version of the dominant nonreligiousness or antireligiousness, a difference of degree more or less coinciding with the split between the politically more moderate Mapai-type social democrat who tends to be more open and less doctrinaire on this as on all other subjects, and the Mapam-type radical Zionists who take the more rigid Marxist ideological view of the matter. These secular-minded Israelis want to re-create the *nation* as the core element of the Jewish identity. For them the nation is the thing. It displaces or at least overrides religion. Some, as socialists, reject religion as the people's opium, while some, as Zionists, reject post-Biblical Judaism as part of the unwanted baggage of the Diaspora. Most of the American settlers in Israel who came over as recruits from Zionist youth organizations belong to one or the other of these two main Zionist groups but tend to be divided when it comes to sharing their characteristic outlooks on religion.

In between these two, in what I would guess a survey would show to be the largest number, are American Jews in Israel who think of themselves as "religious" but not in the Israeli sense of the term at all. They are "religious" in some version of the Orthodox, Conservative, or Reform Jewish persuasions as these are practiced in America, or in some more private way of their own. Many of these Americans are troubled to find themselves outside the pale of Israeli "religious" standards. They find Israeli Orthodoxy barren and resent its control over the society. They are unwilling to be "nothing." They find very little chance to be anything in between, especially if it involves engaging in any form of group worship.

These guesses about the probable distribution of religious attitudes among American Jews in Israel correspond roughly to the guesses that might be made about the Israeli population in general from the findings of a sample survey reported in 1963. This survey suggested that 30 percent of an Israeli population sample was "religious," claiming to be totally or "for the most part" observant; 24 percent "not at all observant, completely secular"; and 46 percent who said they "observe traditions to some extent."* The only other available indicator of this kind is the 15 percent of the popular vote commanded by the various Religious parties in winning seats to the Knesset or Parliament. It is mainly this political power, shrewdly used in Israel's tight coalition politics, that has enabled the Orthodox establishment to impose its version of the

---

* Aaron Antonovsky, "Israeli Political-Social Attitudes," English mimeo. text, published in Hebrew in *Amot*, No. 6, 1963; the gross figures are given by Antonovsky in a letter to *Commentary*, May, 1964.

"Jewish life" on the rest of the population. Officially Israel observes the Sabbath and keeps the food kosher. A fragile balance is kept, the Religious authorities blinking at some necessary maintenance of vital services on the Day of Rest, and the public more or less accepting this system as formally appropriate. But it generates almost constant aggravation and friction, whether between individuals or out in the larger political and social arenas. Orthodox zealots throw rocks at Sabbath violators, and antireligious zealots demonstrate in the streets. The Orthodox establishment keeps up a drumfire of hortatory propaganda aimed at the godless, and the more radical godless band together in a League Against Religious Coercion to press their demand for greater religious freedom. Issues erupt again and again, over what is taught in the schools and how it is taught (the secular schools generally teach the Bible as history and religion as mythology, while the religious schools, also officially supported, teach the Bible as revealed religion), over swimming pools and mixed bathing, over women's dress (or undress), over service in the armed forces, control of dietary observance in the slaughterhouses, over whether the new Israeli liner *Shalom* should have a nonkosher as well as a kosher kitchen, and often most passionately of all, over the validity or nonvalidity of marriages and births and divorces, issues which are sometimes dramatized in single spectacular cases or which sometimes affect whole groups, like the Jews from India known as "B'nei Israel" whose Jewish identity was challenged by the rabbis, or like the mass of recent immigrants from Communist Rumania, or earlier from Poland, virtually none of whom were legally married by Israeli Orthodox standards and whose children are therefore all regarded as illegitimate by the Religious authorities. The latter case suggests what a crisis could be forced in these affairs should the Soviet Union ever lift its bars and allow mass emigration of Soviet Jews to Israel.

American Jews in Israel react to the religious problem in accordance with what kind of Jews they are, and what kind of Zionists. They also react to a remarkable degree, I found, as *Americans,* that is with strongly embedded feelings about separation of church and state and about the right of the individual to practice his religion as his own conscience dictates.

An American businessman I met in Tel Aviv who had come to Israel precisely to be more Orthodox than he had found it possible to be in America was very happy with what he had found in Israel in this respect. He said he agreed in theory with the idea of an inflexible Orthodoxy—he thought this was the only way to be truly religious—and favored the idea that there could and should be only one kind of "Jew," namely the "Jew" as defined by the Israeli rabbinate. He even agreed with one suggestion made to non-Orthodox Jewish groups seeking recognition in Israel: if they would declare themselves to be another religion and stopped calling themselves "Jews" they could have the same rights enjoyed in Israel by Christians and Moslems, but they could not be recognized as dissident or non-Orthodox Jews. He thought that this made good sense, but here he reached his own point of dissent—a peculiarly American kind of dissent: "But I do not approve of government control of religion," he said. "I don't approve of any one group ruling other groups. I don't approve of civil marriage, but I think people are entitled to it if they want it."

At the other end of the spectrum, there were many American Jews who had come to Israel for just the opposite reason, that is, to be "Jews" without being religious at all. Thus a young scholar: "I want to be a Jew and live in a Jewish society. But I am utterly irreligious, therefore it is impossible or difficult to live this way in America. The Gentile holidays are not my holidays. They were not my holidays in the States."

A kibbutznik: "I was not versed in Judaism. I couldn't feel like a positive Jew in any way. In Brooklyn on the holidays we would go to schul [synagogue] because in America if you're religious you can get away with just being a synagogue Jew. But if you're not religious, there's no positive way of expressing the fact that you are a Jew. Here things are different. Here on Shevuoth [the harvest holiday] we have harvest."

A government servant: "I was having a hard time being a valid Jew in America, no trouble being an

American but trouble being a Jew. Maybe you can do this with religion, but I never had religion, so I couldn't do it that way. Jewish religion had no appeal for me, but the Jewish people do. I can do it here, being in the country, building up a Jewish country for Jewish people, something I strongly favor."

For Jews of this kind, the "Jewish life" consisted of the observance of popular Jewish holidays in an all Jewish setting:

"Well, for example, on Succoth back in the States you have a succoh, a little succoh outside. But here every balcony is decorated. You have a wonderful holiday feeling, everybody buying flowers. A real air of simcha, joy. The feeling of being Jewish in a Jewish world, walking down the street and not being different. When your child comes home from school with a black eye or something, you know that it's not because somebody called him a 'dirty Jew.' "

I asked him if that had ever happened to his son, and he said that in fact he didn't have a son and he went on:

"So when the holidays come, kids don't ask your kids, 'What are you doing out of school? Why are you all dressed up?' You see Chanukah menorahs on all the public buildings. It's a good feeling. Regardless of what you believe or observe, to everybody you say, 'Shabat Shalom.' *That's* the Jewish life!"

Again, from an old hand on a kibbutz:

"As for living like a Jew, it is marvelous that I can live through Christmas Day and never know it is

Christmas. In this, Israel has accomplished the task it was supposed to accomplish for all of us."

The holidays mentioned in this way were invariably the more secular national-historic Jewish holidays: Purim, celebrating Esther's victory over Haman; Chanukah, the week of the Maccabean heroes; Passover, the feast of liberation from Egypt. It was possible to reap a great harvest of satisfactions from these occasions, to be "Jewish" without being religious at all.

Times come in the lives of these Jews when they do have to deal with the religious authorities—if they want to be legally married, for example—and this they do with feelings that range from cynical indifference to annoyance to anger to revulsion. There was a bit of all of this in the experience of a young American woman I met on a kibbutz at the edge of the Negev desert. She was not sure what she believed about anything, but had left her home in Scarsdale, New York, because she thought American life was too "materialistic" and she was bothered by the conflict she felt over going to school on Jewish holidays. She came with a youth group to Israel for a year and decided to stay after she fell in love with a type-cast Sabra, muscled, tan, and moustached. They set about getting properly married and it proved to be quite an experience:

"Dealing with the Israelis was really terrible. Everything cost money and it was so unpleasant. I had to get a certificate that I had never been married. In the rabbinical court it is not enough simply to say you had not been married before. You have to bring witnesses or certification. I had to get a letter from our rabbi in Scarsdale and confirming witnesses. And then you also have to prove that your parents were married in a Jewish ceremony! The parents of a friend of mine who was in this same situation came to Israel and got re-married in the Jewish style in order to help their daughter get married. If your parents were not married by a rabbi, you see, then your children could be classified as bastards. It took me three months to get the certificates I needed. We were furious about it all, it was so silly! Here I was, just nineteen years old, and they just didn't believe I'd never been married!"

But if you came to Israel as a "religious" Jew in some American manner—choosing your own way of holding your beliefs and worshipping according to your own version of the Jewish conscience—you faced problems in Israel. How serious this was depended on how seriously you took your religious feelings or your ideas about how the good society deals with it. Conflict between Americans and Europeans on this issue began long ago, even among the young Zionists who came with high socialist zeal to join the kibbutz movement. Here is a report written in 1951 by Ira Eisenstein, a well-known American rabbi:

In one of the kibbutzim, I found that a group of young Americans had agreed to introduce a sort of

[service] at the Friday evening meal. Instead of marking
the Sabbath with merely a white tablecloth and clean
clothes, they wanted to institute the singing of songs
. . . and the recital of some of the traditional Sabbath
service. [It] was a huge success until the Europeans in
that kibbutz began to ridicule it. "What are you doing,"
they asked, "going backward? We gave all that up years
ago. If you want to be religious, why don't you grow
beards and *daven* the whole *davening* [recite all the
ritual prayers]?" Unfortunately the scorn of their fellow
members was more than this group could bear, and
after a week or two, they gave up. The whole project
collapsed. . . . To these people who had come out of
Central and Eastern Europe, religion had to be orthodox
or it was not religion; and religion had to be somehow
involved with the struggle for political power. The
American idea of a free church in a free society, the
liberal notion of a religious tradition which grows and
develops—these were strange and incomprehensible to
them, and so natural, almost axiomatic, to the Americans.*

During my own brief visit twelve years later, I found
the same issues moving the same kind of American
Jews on kibbutzim where in some cases religious services had in fact been revived and continued. One of
the best-known American kibbutzniks in the country
told me:

"It is the Americans who come out of Jewish traditional backgrounds who are now looking for some kind
of new religious basis. They don't accept that you are

* Ira Eisenstein, "Americans in Israel," loc. cit.

either Orthodox or nothing. It's the Americans here on the kibbutz who light candles on Friday nights and don't eat bread at Pesach [Passover] and reproduce some of the traditional elements of the Seder. Some native Israelis do this too, some actively oppose it. But we have even also instituted services here on Rosh Hashonah and Yom Kippur. We have a rabbi come over to officiate."

Another prominent American kibbutznik said:

"Some people here are still fighting God out of their Marxist backgrounds, not just anti-clerical and pro-God, but anti-God. We do have a whole range of agnostics and liberals among us, also a number of convinced and active atheists. But I think where you have a real valid atheist, it's a flaw. This is so anti-historical in a Jew that it raises the whole question of what is Jewishness."

"Religion is important for Jews in America, more important than it is for Jews in Israel, and many of them, when they come here, miss it," said an officer of the Association of Americans and Canadians in Israel whose job it was to help newly arriving immigrants. "They miss what they think of as a Jewish kind of religion. Back home in America, the synagogue is central in their lives. Here this kind of thing is nonexistent. You just go to the synagogue for certain ritualistic observances. Back home, the rabbi is a guide, a kind of chaplain if you will. Here the rabbi is something for *she'elot*, questions about whether something is kosher or not. Nothing personal. Rabbis here are not people who cater to a flock, who work for people who need their wisdom or their help. Religion here is just more impersonal, and many Americans, used to a different kind of thing, don't get along with it all."

To try to fill this need, some American Jews in Israel have tried—along with some non-American Israelis—to establish non-Orthodox congregations of their own. This has proved to be quite a struggle, a much-argued matter not only in Israel—where such efforts are bitterly opposed by the rabbinical establishment—but also in the United States where American Orthodox defenders of Israeli Orthodoxy have just as bitterly opposed American Conservative and Reform efforts to win footholds for their kind of Judaism in Israel.* In Israel at the time of my visit in 1963, there were six struggling non-Orthodox congregations, two Conservative and four Reformed, located in Jerusalem, Tel Aviv, Nazareth, and Haifa. Members included mostly Americans and other "Anglo-Saxons"—English

* E.g., at a 1964 meeting the president of the Orthodox Rabbinical Council of America denounced Reformed Jews for being "disruptive" and divisive" in Israel and asked both Reform and Conservative groups "to desist from any further efforts to bring elements of strife, dissension and disunity into the religious life of Israel."—*New York Times,* November 14, 1964. For a report on a clash on this issue at the 1965 annual meeting of the Zionist Organization of America between an American Orthodox spokesman and several noted Conservative and Reform rabbis who described the situation in Israel as "intolerable," see *New York Times,* July 3, 1965.

and Canadians—and a scattering of other Israelis. The Tel Aviv group, located in the suburb called Kfar Shmaryahu, attempted to rent a hall from the municipality in which to hold their services, but the city authorities refused to let them have it. The group took the case all the way up to the Supreme Court of Israel and won and eventually got their hall.

American rabbis who come to Israel suffer peculiarly sharp pangs not only over the religious situation in general but over their own status in the country. I met one such young rabbi who had found a job in which he could be helpful to people who needed help. He said: "In general American Jews find themselves out in the cold religiously. Rabbis who come here from America are working at other jobs. As rabbis they are out in the cold too. They have no way to participate. They are not allowed to perform ordinary rabbinical functions. When they come here, they work at all sorts of jobs. We have just organized an informal committee of six of these rabbis working in various places. Some of them are Orthodox in the American sense, but they are not as religious as the Israeli Orthodox require. Some of them have even gone into businesses! But not one of them is functioning as a rabbi. They would not function here as rabbis anyway because rabbis are held in such low esteem in Israel, they couldn't stand it. A purely ritualistic functionary, supported by the Ministry of Religion! The Orthodox in Israel are not so unlike some American Orthodox, but the main difference is that they get themselves into politics and act primarily as a political party, not as religious leaders. We Americans don't think of this as a way of being religious."

He said the six non-Orthodox congregations in the country were "poorly organized and have no leadership." They cannot have proper rabbis of their own, since non-Orthodox rabbis are not officially recognized and therefore cannot perform marriages or preside at funerals, or any other such functions. Moreover, he went on rather sadly, the push from the groups themselves was not as strong as it had to be. "Unfortunately the Conservative or Reformed person is by definition not a zealot. If they pushed hard there would be a great opportunity. But there are all kinds of obstacles. They will continue to have trouble finding a place to hold services and will have to raise a lot of money to build their own synagogue—there won't be any government support for them! And also men in public positions or those who depend on proper connections for their affairs tend to keep away from a thing like this because it might not be too healthy for them to belong to it. I'm talking about Americans now. In fact, strong influence is used to try to keep people away from this synagogue group—somebody approached its youth leader and tried to get him to stop being active in it."

He had mixed and worried feelings about the state of religion in Israel. "It's the whole climate in Israel, the attitude about religion in general is negative. Here you're Orthodox or you're nothing. The close relationship between religion and politics has had a bad effect on religion in general. When it becomes part of a larger Jewish culture, the religious life suffers. Maybe this is a natural thing. Maybe if you live in a Jewish society, religion becomes less important. Here an Israeli often finds the Jewish part of his identity completely unnecessary." The Jewish part? I asked. "I mean the religious part," he explained. "To me religion is essential to being Jewish, to the Israeli it is not. Judaism for many Sabras is identified purely with the ritual aspect, just the ritual aspect. It has nothing to do with the moral and ethical aspects. These things are completely divorced from what they identify as religious. There are simply those who wear the *kipa* [skullcap] and observe the rituals. That is being religious. I think the failure of religion to play more of a role here is having a profound effect on the morals of this society." He went on to catalogue a series of examples, referring to the "cutthroat, frontier mentality" which dominated much of the common behavior among people, and to the lack of values his children found when he sent them to a religious school. "I want to temper all this," he went on uncomfortably, "for I feel this may all be inevitable because of the pressures Israel is subject to—maybe this is all unavoidable and must simply take time. There are still more things right here than wrong. I have a firm conviction by the faith I have in the strength of Judaism, things will get better here, not worse. But the things I see that are wrong here bother me. I didn't come with illusions, but it bothers me that things exist here that I don't think ought to exist in a Jewish state. My orientation on religion is completely different from what I find here."

He said his own year in Israel had been an experiment. He was rabbi of a Conservative congregation in a small American city and there were things about it that had led him to take a year off to see what it was like in Israel. But what he had seen was sending him back to his small-town synagogue in America.

"I had considered staying here," he said, "but I am definitely going back. I have been a rabbi for fifteen years and it's very frustrating to try to build a positive Jewish way of living in America. I think I would come here to stay if I felt there was a more positive Jewish life here, or even if I could see that I could do something about it here. But I would never consider being a rabbi here. The only way I could stay here would be to go into business or something, and I couldn't do that." He shook his head with a rueful kind of sadness. "The truth is that I have found that America is more conducive to living religiously than Israel is."

The Holy Land is not entirely barren, however, of some new religious growth. More meaningful reaches are being made for some new Jewish religious self-expression, one is told, quite outside the framework of organized persuasion. There is "a crisis of values" and a "yearning for something," a way of filling the emptiness in an environment where one is otherwise "Orthodox or nothing." Among Israeli intellectuals there is a certain ferment over the issues of the moral and religious content of the country's life. Among some young people, who are described as being people given neither to books nor to words, there is said to be a certain banding together in search of some new Jewish spirituality. Herbert Weiner describes several such groups in *The Wild Goats of Ein Gedi*. I heard an account from a veteran settler who told me, with great relish, of a group of young people on a particularly doctrinaire type of kibbutz, who went through with a football game which had been scheduled—not accidentally—on Yom Kippur, the Day of Atonement, holiest day in the Jewish religious calendar. But even though they played, they fasted, and later went out into the woods where they spent the rest of the day reading the Bible and meditating. These were not Americans, but Eastern European Israeli-born youngsters. Their parents, my informant delightedly told me, were left speechless by this act of rebellion.

He went on to tell me about a group in which he was taking part himself, a "Chavurah" or simply "comradeship" or "community," in which a number of people had come together to commune among themselves on all these matters. "We are trying to keep down the number of Americans in it," he said self-consciously. "We want it to be indigenously Israeli. About one quarter of its members are Germans, some are Eastern European Sabras, and a few Iraqis." They have not organized themselves in any formal way—that could get troublesome. But they do meet at regular intervals, usually on Friday nights, and although they are careful not to call it a religious service, they do read a weekly portion from the Bible, as is usually done on the Sabbath. Then they have a discussion, seeking to clarify their thinking about the problem of religion and what is often commonly called "the crisis of values" in Israel. They will talk, for example, about the much-debated "Jewish consciousness," a subject introduced by the Zionist leadership into Israel's public school curriculum as an ill-defined response to the feeling shared by many that the youth are suffering somehow from a lack of genuine spirituality and from the effects of negative attitudes toward the Jewish traditions associated with the 2,000 years of the Diaspora. It is a small group and is part of a minor current in Israeli life that some hope—optimistically— will become its mainstream some time in the future. Meanwhile American Jews who have feelings about these matters have to settle for what they can get out of life in Israel as they find it now.

"There *is* a half-way between being Orthodox and being nonreligious," insisted an American settler in

Jerusalem. "Most Americans are not Orthodox and their forms of religion are not available here. Americans have to content themselves with the fact that it's a Jewish country, using the Hebrew language, oriented to the Bible which is taught in the schools, where there is no non-Jewish world, where the holidays are only Jewish holidays. You don't have to feel religious to feel the Sabbath in Israel. Everything just stops here. The stores are closed and so on. To see the empty streets here on Yom Kippur is to realize just how Jewish this society is. To travel where the Bible was living history —this is what one has to content himself with! To have a sense of participation in all this—that's the *important* thing!"

To be participating in building a Jewish state, to be taking part in history, to be able to say, as one so warmly did say: "This is mine!"—this was the important thing indeed. But *participation* involved a whole great cluster of other nettles that Americans in Israel had to grasp. They had come to Israel to *belong* and *belonging* meant becoming part of the new Jewish state and to take full part in the new Jewish State of Israel, it was necessary to commit oneself to it fully. This turned out for many to be the most troubling nettle of all. Religion or Jewishness was not the crux of their problem of identity as American Jews in Israel; it was nationality. Being *Jews* was not the most painful of their problems; it was becoming *Israelis*.

8. Becoming "Israelis"

The "private agony" of a large number of American Jews in Israel is wrapped up in the uniquely American, peculiarly private, and quietly agonizing question of citizenship. American Jews who go to Israel to live have to choose whether to remain Americans or to become Israelis. This does not mean choosing to remain Americans by background, education, or sentiment, or guiding ideas, or becoming Israelis by attachment and interest. It means choosing literally and formally whether to remain American citizens or to become *Israelis,* citizens of Israel. This is uniquely a problem for Americans because, unlike many other countries, the United States does not allow its citizens to hold dual citizenship in another nation. If American Jews entered Israel as "olim," or immigrants, under the Law of Return they would, like all other returning Jews, acquire Israeli citizenship automatically, by the fact of being Jews and by the act of returning. To avoid this, they must declare expressly on arrival that they are not olim but are coming to Israel to be "tem-

porary residents." When, as, and if they become
"permanent residents," they must "opt out" of Israeli
citizenship. They must explicitly retain their American citizenship. Whether they are temporary residents
or permanent residents, this is what the great majority
of American Jews in Israel have done.

"There is no way of knowing just how many Americans have become Israeli citizens," said one of the best-
informed Americans in the country. "We simply do
not have these facts." The lowest estimate I was given
of the number of citizens was "between 600 and 700."
The best-informed Americans I met used terms like
"small" or "not many" or "negligible." Several of them
offered a guess of "about 10 percent" as a probable
outside proportion of citizens in the American population in Israel. If there were in fact "about 10,000"
Americans in Israel, this meant that there were "about
1,000" citizens among them. This was not a verifiable
figure, only an indication of magnitude.*

During my journey of inquiry, I came upon Israeli
citizens mainly among the more veteran American

* A radically higher figure was supplied more recently by David Breslau,
president of the Association of Americans and Canadians in Israel, in
letters to the author dated November 19 and December 26, 1966. He said
that "as of 1965 based on a survey conducted by the A.A.C.I.," there
were 3,700 American-born and Canadian-born Israeli citizens, and more,
still uncounted, among European-born immigrants from these two
countries. Breslau's total for American and Canadian born in Israel is
6,900, which he says is by actual count. His total for Americans and
Canadians in Israel is 20,000, in which he includes all individuals who
ever lived in the United States or Canada for at least five years. The
usual proportion of Canadians in such figures is 10 percent. By this
account, therefore, more than half of all American-born Americans in
Israel are Israeli citizens. If this was a fact when I was interviewing
Americans in Israel in 1963, it was extraordinarily well hidden from all

settlers on the kibbutzim where Zionist motivation and group pressures and sanctions are characteristically strong. Among the city dwellers I met who had become Israelis, several were older-timers who had come to Palestine before the Second World War, some were ex-kibbutzniks who had come originally as young Zionist recruits, and a few were men who had come to fight for the state in the war against the Arabs in 1948. None of these categories, however, could be taken to have any consistent patterns. I also met older-timers, ex-kibbutzniks, 1948 war veterans, and even some Zionist kibbutzniks who were still holding very firmly to their American passports, even though some of them had been in Israel for as long as fifteen years, and I was told of others who had been around even longer without ever becoming citizens of the new state.

A certain small number of Americans who came to Israel before some of these particular definitions were fixed in both countries by law (in 1952) still unofficially enjoy a mixed kind of status; they automatically became Israeli citizens but never gave up their American citizenship. If they are careful how they deal with

---

the best-informed authorities I was able to find, including Mr. Breslau, the then officers of the A.A.C.I., officials at the U.S. Embassy, and many others. If every other American in Israel was in fact a citizen, I am at a loss to understand why so many veteran settlers, deeply concerned with the problems of American immigrants, should have without exception told me that only a small minority of Americans had become Israeli citizens and that this was the source of some acutely felt problems among them. If there has been any unusual rush of Americans to become citizens in Israel since 1963, it is no less difficult to see how this could have gone unnoticed and unreported until now. Verification of these figures will have to wait for publication of the details of the A.A.C.I. survey.

the formalities as they arise, they can manage to hold on to both. There are others who came in the fine glow of those early days, arrived as olim, accepted Israeli citizenship as a benediction, and presented themselves at the nearest American consulate to renounce their American citizenship—I will come to a vivid description of that experience—but this hardly ever happens now. At the American Embassy in Tel Aviv I was told there might be "two or three" such cases in a year. No one I asked was able to cite any known examples of any Americans coming in recent years as olim under the Law of Return. At the Jewish Agency, the official in charge of immigration from Western countries said flatly that all Americans who have entered the country in recent years—"and I mean *all*," he emphasized, "this is no exaggeration"—have entered as "temporary residents" and retained their American citizenship. Under Israeli law one can remain a "temporary resident" only for three years. In fact, this is extended by various maneuvers, sometimes indefinitely. I was told there were some "temporary residents" who have held on to that classification for ten years or more—they are often scornfully referred to as "permanent temporary residents" or "temporary permanents."* When every possible extension of the "temporary" status has been exhausted, the "temporary resident" goes through a

* Precise official figures on this, as on other things, are hard to come by in Israel. A well-informed authority suggested in a 1964 article that "frontier-control authorities estimate that the number of these 'temporary

formidable bureaucratic procedure to become a "permanent resident," a status carrying with it certain important changes in legal position—a permanent resident is, for example, liable to military service—but leaving the matter of citizenship untouched. This is why most Americans in Israel shy away from the term "oleh." They do not want to be called "immigrants" and they cannot even conscientiously call themselves "settlers"—the English word most often used as equivalent for "olim." They remain simply "residents" and mostly "temporary residents" at that. They are outsiders who have come to Israel to be insiders, but once inside Israel *opt out*—that is, they choose to remain outsiders. It is not surprising, then, that for many of these individuals this choice becomes a private and, for many, an agonizing matter.

How very "private" it was, I discovered in the first conversations I had with Americans in Israel when I was trying to find out just how many Americans there were in the country. As I indicated earlier, it became necessary first to define what an "American" was in

---

permanents' from Western countries now stands at 13,000." This figure includes both those who are technically "tourists"—i.e., people who manage to extend their stay on tourist visas—and "temporary residents" and it is also not clear whether he is using "Western countries" simply as a euphemism for the United States. In any case, since this same author gives "10,400" as the total figure for American immigration into Israel since the creation of the state, he is obviously including among the estimated 13,000 "temporary permanents" a substantial number of "tourists" and perhaps some uncertain number of Western Europeans who have also chosen this in-between status, or what this writer calls "pseudo-aliya." See Lapide, "American Aliya, Past Facts and Future Hopes," loc. cit.

this context. During this process of definition, the question of citizenship popped out quite innocently and I suddenly discovered that it was a touchy and sensitive matter, like asking a person about his sex habits or the size of his income. "This is a delicate question," cautioned one of my first informants, an American who had held on to his American citizenship. "You don't ask. Why, I don't know among my own friends who has and who hasn't—given up their passports, that is. I suspect that most of them are still American citizens. But I don't ask. It's one of those delicate personal things you just don't inquire about."

I heard this again more than once as I pursued my initial inquiries. When shortly thereafter I met my first American Israeli, I pressed him harder to describe the situation. He gave me an outline of it, going only reluctantly into details, and making me assure him more than once that I would not quote him by name on the subject. I asked him if there were any printed sources I could go to, and he shook his head. He said: "Somehow critical issues like this don't get written up by anyone. I think it would be a good idea if somebody did write about it. But not me. I wouldn't touch it. It's a hard thing to explain away. It would be highly controversial, and a lot of people would say: 'You shouldn't have written about this.' But I'd be glad if somebody did. An awful lot of people simply don't want to look at it. They are afraid to face it."

I asked every American I interviewed in Israel how he faced this matter of citizenship, and though I was

not quite made to feel like a Kinsey interviewer when-
ever the talk came around to this subject, I always
knew I was on tender ground, whether I was with an
American who "had" or "had not"—given up his passport, that is. A few of those who had kept their passports were cynical about it. Others either tried to
ignore the question or to change the subject as quickly
as they could. Most commonly, the style was to brush it
aside as "unimportant," to minimize it as a "mere
formality" or "just a technicality," to explain it on
"practical" grounds, or otherwise to rationalize it,
using a whole collection of obviously well-worn formulas. But no American I met who had become an Israeli
citizen thought the subject could be ignored, or that it
was unimportant or merely technical. The citizens I
met spoke of the noncitizens almost invariably with
sympathy or charity, sometimes with censure but more
often with pity, and also with a weary kind of sorrow, a
sorrow for those others, but also a little, it sometimes
seemed, for themselves.

The Hard Choices

Americans in Israel are just about the only people
there who have to face the problem of making a choice
in the matter of their citizenship. It is one of their
uniquenesses as Americans they would be glad to forgo
if they could only be relieved of the need to choose, to
commit themselves.

The great mass of Israelis, of course, had no such

choice at all. Large numbers of them were stateless Europeans. Many left or fled from countries in which they had only the most fragile or limited rights as citizens or none at all. They abandoned nationalities they no longer wanted or never had. By becoming Israelis these Jews from Eastern and Central Europe, and even more so, the Jews from northern Africa, Egypt, and such countries as Iraq or Yemen, acquired the first real nationality they had ever had. On the other hand, the much smaller numbers of Jews who came to Israel from the Commonwealth countries, Western Europe, and Latin America usually did hold citizenship status in those countries and could generally, under their laws, hold dual citizenship and carry two passports. This was subject in the British case to some limits where naturalized citizens were concerned, and in the South African case was coming, at the time of my visit to Israel, under certain new pressures following on South Africa's withdrawal from the Commonwealth. But most commonly, these migrants could become Israeli citizens while still remaining citizens of the countries from which they came, enjoying whatever advantages were available from this double identification and double acceptance.*

Not so the Americans. The Walter-McCarran Act of

* A veteran American settler's view of Commonwealth Israelis: "The British and the others are different from the Americans. The South Africans are coming now out of need, out of fear of the explosions they think are coming in their country on the black-white issue. In any case, the South Africans are much more Jewish. There is no third generation to speak of in South Africa, and they have deeper roots in the Zionist movement. The English come out of an entirely different psychological setting compared to the Americans. The British Jews were apparently

1952 spelled out details that had previously been vague in American citizenship law. It specifically barred Americans from serving in a foreign army, voting in a foreign election, or entering the regular employ of a foreign government—all, subject to certain exceptions, under penalty of forfeiture of American citizenship.*

---

never really at home in England. If anybody asks them what they are, they would say: I am a British Jew. The American, when first asked what he is, would naturally say: I am an American. The English and the Americans here don't get on very well. You rarely have English and Americans together. The cultural difference separates them. Americans are a lot closer to the Sabras in their outlook, raised in freedom, brusque but friendly. The British are not like this. The British do not however have the citizenship problem that we have since Britain recognizes dual citizenship. It is a somewhat different matter with the South Africans in the sense that if any of them leave here to 'go back,' they won't go back to South Africa but to the U.K. or to the U.S. They never felt themselves to be part of South Africa the way Americans feel themselves to be part of America."

A self-glimpse from the secretary of the British Settlers Association: "We are not as spoiled as the Americans. Britishers [sic] are more used to difficult conditions. Those who do go back—and we share with Americans the privilege of having a country to go back to—usually do so for purely economic reasons. We don't think that Britishers are as aggravated by things like plumbing. We are more patient about such things. I would say that 99 percent of us carry both British and Israeli passports. You can't do this if you are naturalized, but most English citizens in Israel do enjoy the best of both worlds."

The secretary of the Israel office of the South African Zionist Federation explained that the new South African citizenship law (aimed at South African holders of British passports) created certain problems for South African holders of Israeli passports, but that a way had been found around the difficulty. South Africans still *do* feel they can go back to South Africa, he said, but those who can—if they had a British father holding British citizenship—are switching to British passports.

* The reader is reminded here that all references in these pages to the legal restraints on Americans in Israel in the matter of citizenship have to be read now in the past tense instead of the present. By a decision handed down on May 29, 1967, the United States Supreme Court ruled that the Congress did not have the power to pass laws depriving Americans of their nationality without their consent. It was not clear whether this decision would allow Americans hereafter to hold dual citizenship, but the ruling did clearly invalidate the citizenship provisions of the Walter-McCarran Act of 1952 and all similar legislation. This created a new legal situation for American Jews in Israel, freeing them from the

Thus what had been legal, or at least not illegal, for the Americans who flew for France before 1917 or for China before Pearl Harbor, or fought in Allenby's Jewish Brigade against the Turks in 1916–1918, or in Israel's army against the Arabs in 1948, became illegal after 1952. It is this law, as many Americans in Israel see it, that creates their painful dilemma, and they blame it, rather than their own ambivalence, for their acute discomfort. "When will America get mature enough to allow dual citizenship?" testily asked one American caught on the hard horns of his dilemma in Israel. Actually Americans are caught between the legal requirements of both nationalities, the one they want not quite to abandon, and the other they want not quite to embrace. For on the Israeli, as well as on the American side, this is not merely a matter of feeling but also of law.

Chief among anyone's national obligations in today's world is military service, and all Americans of military age in Israel have to thread their way through assorted American and Israeli requirements. Most American Jews who have migrated to Israel in these years have either satisfied their military obligations at home or else remain in proper contact with their draft boards through registration at the American consulates in

most explicit and formal aspects of the citizenship dilemma described in this report. For a brief discussion of the impact of this decision and the impact of the war crisis in Israel, during which it came, the reader is referred to the Prefatory Note, which was added to this book as it was going to press.

Israel. There were a few sticky cases back in the early 1950s when a small number of Americans came to Israel partly in flight from what they thought was becoming a McCarthyist America, and partly to evade service in the Korean War, and as a result fell afoul of the draft law and forfeited their citizenship. In "three or four" of those cases, an Embassy official told me, there were later painful second thoughts and special action was instituted to allow the individuals concerned to return to the United States. By a Supreme Court decision in February, 1963,* the previous administrative procedure was disallowed, and the consulate would in such cases now issue a limited one-way passport to any accused draft evader to enable him to stand trial on the charge at home. But there have been no such cases in recent years, as far as I could learn. After the unpleasantnesses of the early 1950s, the Zionist youth groups in the United States generally required their recruits to satisfy their American military

* In a case of an individual who had gone abroad to evade the draft, the Court found that deprivation of citizenship in such cases could only follow due process through trial and conviction.—*New York Times*, February 18, 1963. This decision, reported in the press while I was in Israel, was immediately interpreted by some Americans there as meaning that the American authorities could no longer act administratively against Americans charged with serving in the Israeli armed forces but would have to refer any such cases back home for court action. An Embassy official pointed out, when I asked him about this, that the decision referred only to cases of draft evasion. The law incurring loss of citizenship for taking part in a foreign election was upheld by the Court in a 1958 case. In 1964, in a test case involving an American who had served with Castro's army in Cuba, the Court affirmed that service in a foreign army did incur loss of citizenship. These were among the previous Court rulings reversed by the decision of May 29, 1967.

obligations before going to Israel. In the case of other migrants, there has rarely ever been any question about any action contrary to American law in these matters. "All the Americans registered with us are very careful about this," the responsible consular official at the Tel Aviv embassy told me. "They come in here and register properly. When a boy reaches age eighteen here, he faces a choice if he is an American citizen. He either has to register with us for the draft at home, or answer the Israeli call to service. We have about twenty or thirty a year like this who come in here and register with us. Most of these are students who are here temporarily, for a year or so, but a few might be the sons of residents."

Israeli law, for its part, requires all persons between the ages of eighteen and thirty-seven permanently residing in the country, whether citizens or not, to serve in the armed forces, with certain obligations to the reserve up to ages forty-five or forty-nine. Sons and daughters of Americans in Israel who reach age eighteen are faced at that point with *their* formal choice. With very rare exceptions, I was told, they opt *in,* go off to the army, and thereby nullify the claim to American citizenship which their parents have often carefully preserved for them by preserving their own status as American citizens. This is sometimes the occasion for painful conflict. One veteran settler said:

"There are some Americans who have been here twenty years and are still American citizens. They register their children as Americans. When these children grow up and go into the army, of course they lose this citizenship. But their parents have abstained all this time from both the army and from voting. The children are confused by this and in many cases there has been high tension created in families when children discover, often in their late teens, what their parents have been doing. They accuse their parents of letting others take care of their needs when the hard times come. You can see what a sensitive thing this is."

Americans who have become Israeli citizens automatically meet these obligations as they arise. They do their regular stint, and then a month in the reserves each year; when a crisis occurs, they go off to serve again on call. Since Israel is under such constant threat around all its borders, military service is never merely a routine matter.

Americans who have not become Israeli citizens but who are eligible for military service have to meet these demands one way or another. Many Americans are of course not legally affected, including all who are too old and the large numbers who may be young enough but as "temporary residents" are not legally subject to call. This leaves some small number who are both of military age and are, as "permanent residents," legally required to serve. Some few such eligibles find indirect ways around the difficulty. If they are kibbutzniks, they can often satisfy their military obligations "unofficially," since many kibbutzim are in frontier areas and have certain special status as defense positions. There are said to be some non-Israeli Americans who manage to serve in the Israeli armed forces but are able to keep this fact off their official records. But for the great bulk of these eligibles, it is a matter of not serving at all. This is accomplished with the informal agreement of the Israeli military authorities. Eligible Americans are exempted from serving simply because they are Americans who do not wish to jeopardize their American citizenship—a special kind of 4F-ness in Israel that leaves these Americans with a feeling of considerable discomfort. Israeli authorities, I was told, have been growing more and more reluctant to continue making this special dispensation for Americans. "Suppose a Moroccan or anybody else who is called up objects and says, 'What about the Americans, if I have to serve, why don't they?'—what do we say to him?" asked an Israeli official with whom I discussed this problem. "We can't go on indefinitely making special exceptions for the Americans. It gets harder and harder to see why they should have any special position compared to anyone else." A year or so after the time of my visit, I have been told, informal soundings were taken to see whether the Israeli military would accept eligible Americans on some kind of informal or nonformal basis that would satisfy their consciences but would not become a matter of record. There was apparently not much impulse on the part of the Israeli military authorities, however, to find any new formula for relieving the Americans' discomfort.

Much more direct pressure has been put on the 300-odd Americans working in Israel as government servants. Here again, the Israeli government made a special dispensation for those who wanted to remain American citizens. All American employees were put on a "contractual" basis, a status which satisfied the requirements of the American law. But Israeli feeling has changed, partly about the indispensability of these American government workers, but mainly about Israeli's own national sensibilities. In 1959, in an action apparently aimed directly at this group of Americans, a law was passed not unreasonably requiring all servants of the Israeli government to be Israeli citizens. This started quite a wrestling match. The upshot was that enforcement of the law was not immediately pressed, but the extensions in recent years have been negotiated with greater and greater difficulty. As each man's contract comes up, or as each new year's arrangements are made in the various ministries and bureaus, the issue has to be confronted again, and decided again. It persists as an unpleasant irritant in each one's relations with his superiors and his fellow officials, particularly with American fellow officials who have become citizens and don't have the problem, and perhaps most of all, in each one's relations with himself.

I came quite accidentally on one of these testing moments myself one day when I was in the office of an American working for the government, a veteran of the war in 1948 who had, however, retained his American citizenship. As one who had come to fight at the crucial time, he could and obviously did feel that he had committed more personally to Israel than many others. Still, it was not simple to carry it through. He had been talking to me of the element of nostalgia in the lives of Americans in Israel—an English-language program on Radio Israel catered to their needs by playing Dorsey tunes and the scores of the latest Broadway musicals as well as the scores of the day's ball games. He remarked that this was the special position and the special difficulty Americans had: they could not only go back in memory to things they cherished, but could also go back physically, any time they wanted to do so. This is what made it different for them in Israel. He looked out the window for a moment and then turned and said: "I would say that the ones who really get by here are the ones who give up their citizenship." He looked at me quizzically. "It's not a very high percentage, you know." Then he rose abruptly. "As a matter of fact, I'm going to have to settle this myself, right now. I'm due downstairs at half past twelve. They are going to tell me I have to give up my citizenship by April or lose my job." I asked what he was going to tell them downstairs. "I'm going to tell them to go to hell," he said.

It is easier for the American citizen not to vote than it is for him to abstain from military service or to insist on remaining a non-Israeli while working for the Israeli government. Israel's exposed and dangerous situation makes abstention from military service an embarrassingly glaring example of personal noncommitment. Having to confront one's superiors periodically on the citizenship issue is an unpleasant ordeal in which this degree of noncommitment must be openly asserted and defended again and again. But the act of nonparticipation by not voting is a more passive and generally a less visible act, made easier for some by their dissatisfaction with the nature and style of Israeli politics.

On the other hand, American Jews who have come to Israel say they have come *to take part* in the making of a Jewish state. That is why they left America; it was their way of *doing something* about their beliefs. When they get to Israel and then refuse to put themselves in a position to take part, to do anything about anything in the public affairs of the country, they create an anomaly which may be somewhat less painful than avoiding military service but it is nevertheless considerably less than comfortable. So it, too, becomes a "private" matter about which people prefer not to talk.

Whatever his discomfort, however, the city-dwelling non-Israeli American can fail to vote at election time and it can remain a private matter between himself and his own feelings. Not so the kibbutzniks. In politics, as in virtually every other aspect of their lives, kibbutzniks live in the glass bowl of their little enclosed communities. Kibbutzim are products of Zionist ideology and this ideology is focused on the Jewish state; to be a Zionist-kibbutznik and a noncitizen of Israel is an anomaly not easily maintained on the kibbutz in the face of the common disapproval. Kibbutzim, moreover, are highly political institutions. Each one is part of a political party establishment. They are parts of a political machine and one major business of political machines is to get out the vote at election time. Indeed, for many kibbutzim it is rather crucial that they deliver all the votes they can. This makes voting time a time of trial for the noncitizen kibbutznik.

"On the kibbutz," explained a leading kibbutznik, "these commitments are much harder to dodge. In the city you can be an island. Here it is harder. It is important for the kibbutz to get out its vote. This is a Mapai kibbutz and this means, in contrast to our Mapam opponents, that our members can pay dues and vote for other parties if they want to—in the last election 10 of our 120 votes went to other parties. This is bad enough from the standpoint of our party organization, but the important thing is the size of our vote. If, for example, only 75 of our 120 voted, it would be most unfortunate. It would be very embarrassing to us. You know how it is in politics, connections count. If you are dealing with the government in arranging credit or other affairs of the kibbutz, and the guy at the desk where you go is a member of your party, it helps. There are ways of being either tougher or easier in some of the details of the arrangements that have to be made. Getting papered up for these things is quite a job in Israel and if you come from a politically strong kibbutz, it doesn't make it harder. So if we have some people who don't vote because they are still American citizens, we have to explain, we have to tell them at headquarters that we still have some Americans who have not acclimatized themselves to the country and this isn't pleasant to do or very helpful."

So at election time, political workers move around the tight little kibbutz to get the voters out to the polls and to put the pressure on the laggards. "They came around to get me down to the polls," one American woman recounted. "But I said I couldn't vote, that I wasn't on the voters list. They knew it all right and what they came for, I got—a thorough lecture for failing in my obligations." European members of the kibbutz did not get along particularly well with the

Americans and were glad to push hard on the issue of citizenship—which at this kibbutz involved only two or three individual Americans—as a way of expressing their feelings about Americans in general. They kept bringing the matter up in the kibbutz council, she said, and a motion on the subject was coming up again shortly in the Committee on Ideological and Personal Problems. On another kibbutz similarly where I was informed that there were "10 to 15" members who had retained their American citizenship, European members of the kibbutz were trying to win adoption of a rule requiring anyone who had lived on the kibbutz longer than three years to renounce any foreign nationality. "They have strong feelings about it," said a leading American member. "They accuse Americans who keep their citizenship of wanting to have a place to run to in case of trouble, but this is not so, it is not so at all. During the Sinai campaign, when the American Embassy asked all Americans to evacuate, nobody left from here, no regular members, only one couple who were candidates for membership. They made a lot out of that. But I think they are wrong in trying to make a rule out of this. I think it is a matter of private conscience." A woman kibbutznik told me: "We have a lot of fighting here over this business of citizenship, some quiet, some not so quiet. It's the idea that on the kibbutz above all one must show love of country and fulfill all the hardest conditions of doing one's bit, for the kibbutz and for the country too. They think it improper to live in Israel, and especially to live on a kibbutz, and not to vote or serve in the army."

The Association of Americans and Canadians in Israel does its best to keep clear of the sharp horns of these dilemmas. In back files of its *Bulletin* in a summer issue in 1959 I came on a letter from a reader complaining about a paragraph that had apparently appeared in a previous issue under the heading "Helpful Hints" and which gave instructions to newcomers on how to avoid Israeli citizenship. The letter writer asked the editor "to give information on how to become an Israeli citizen, since becoming an Israeli is the obvious end and consequence of settling in Israel." To this the editor replied: "It is not the policy of the Association to interfere in the individual's decision with regard to his citizenship status. We are always ready to furnish information to any member who inquires at our office as to his rights and privileges as an American citizen or as to his rights and privileges as an Israeli citizen."*

In 1961 the issue was forced into the open for a time when some members asked that the Association change its English name to "American-Canadian Settlers Association," bringing it into agreement with the name as given in Hebrew. This forced the "temporary resi-

---

* *Bulletin* of the AACI, August, 1959.

dents" to resist, since the proposed name would exclude them. Possibly because many could not speak or read Hebrew well and some not at all, their identification as "settlers" in Hebrew apparently did not bother them, but they could not accept it in English. Supporters of the proposal indicated that it was precisely their purpose to force everyone to decide whether to be insiders or outsiders. "By obdurately remaining outsiders," wrote an officer of the Jerusalem section of the Association in a letter to the *Bulletin,* "peering from a distance, as it were, at the local scene, we have forfeited our right to participate in Israeli affairs, express opinions, and act on issues of social importance facing this country."* The same writer was fighting the same battle in another letter three years later: "I realize that many of our members, particularly those uninclined to root themselves in Israel, are unwilling to have the organization get embroiled in what they term 'political issues,' but in the last analysis everything in this country is political. . . . I think that we have something to say and something to do about such matters as the right to civil marriage, the need for electoral reform . . . the need to abolish the party key in high civil service . . . the right of non-orthodox rabbis to recognition. . . . Many of our more timid members, particularly the permanent temporary residents, maintain that if we take a stand on

* *Bulletin* of the AACI, March–April, 1961, p. 28.

such issues, we will estrange part of our membership; but the facts remain that by failing to take such a stand, we are estranging others."*

At the 1963 convention of the Association which I attended, the issue of citizenship flickered a few times during the proceedings but was quickly snuffed out. A resolution was brought in calling upon the AACI "to encourage its members to assume full citizenship in order that they may play a more significant role in the development of the country." It was adopted, but hurriedly and with no discussion. At the end of a long session where there had been much airing of complaints about the Jewish Agency and the manifold problems of getting along in Israeli society, one woman suddenly remarked: "One source of our trouble is the anomalous position we are in. We are not really *olim,* but tourists or temporary residents. This creates a problem." There were a few seconds of silence as these words hung in the air, but then the fan of the argument resumed and they were blown away beyond further hearing. A little later a kibbutznik member interrupted to say: "Everyone here is presenting his own grievances. We should be thinking of the larger problems." There seemed to be a very palpable awareness in the group of the differences separating the kibbutzniks from the city dwellers, differences of ideology and commitment and general attitudes, and also more particularly differences of immediate preoccupation: the

* *Bulletin* of the AACI, January–February, 1964, p. 11.

kibbutzniks did not have the problems of jobs, housing, language, schooling, bureaucratic headaches, with which all the city dwellers had to deal. This made for differences and a certain brittleness in mutual dealings. The kibbutznik in this particular argument pressed his point: "We don't have only these problems here," he insisted, "but also the psychological hardship of forgetting you are Americans and becoming Israelis!" Again, these words hovered for a moment over the gathering and again the talk wafted them away, tumbling on past the issue which did not appear again but remained there, uneasily unspoken, just under the surface of everyone's thought.

The Americans who choose not to become Israeli citizens have to meet these pressures on them, whether from the outside or from within themselves. Most of them do so more or less consistently. They keep their passports and their registration in order, they take the exemption from military service, they do not vote, and they insist, if they work for the government, on retaining their "contractual" status. Among such government servants, if the pressure gets too great—as it evidently has in a number of cases involving security positions or representation abroad—the individual is forced to decide, he succumbs or resigns. In the case of military service, as we have already suggested, some individuals do manage to serve anyway and find ways of avoiding the consequences. Similarly in the case of voting, a few vote anyway, thereby violating both Israeli and American laws. The Israeli electoral system can apparently absorb a noncitizen voter, especially if his vote is cast on a kibbutz. But to keep the fact of his vote from the American authorities, this individual has to take steps.

Everyone resident in Israel, citizen or not, carries an identity card. When a person votes, his card is stamped with that fact, an elementary way of assuring that no one votes more than once. The American who votes and has his card stamped knows that the next time he has occasion to go to the American Embassy or a consulate for any service, he will be asked for his card and if it tells the tale of his voting, he will have problems. Such cards are therefore usually "lost" sometime between the election and the next visit to the consulate. This can be quite a long interval, since passports have to be renewed only every three years, and some Americans in Israel let them lapse, coming in to get regularized again only when they need a passport to travel. When they do come in, however, they have been through a long Israeli bureaucratic mill to replace their "lost" cards, and they usually have a clean and stampless card to show. This does not, however, seem to happen very often. Very few Americans are said to choose this way of trying to enjoy the best of their two worlds. "The great majority of Americans who remain American citizens do it clean," a well-informed American Israeli said. "They don't violate the law in any way at all." A responsible official at the American consulate-general in Tel Aviv had the same opinion. "I think there are very few deliberate liars or people trying to conceal their acts," he said, "though I have no doubt there are some. We know about it, and we have been closing these loopholes pretty steadily. There aren't many and they will get fewer and fewer." He went on to explain the procedure followed when a violation was found:

"When anybody comes in here for any kind of service, we look at his identity card and we check up on them especially when they are young people. If we find they have joined the army or voted, we issue a certificate of loss of citizenship which is sent to Washington where the State Department registers this person as having lost his American citizenship. Also if you work for the government, you are liable to the same action, but if you are a contractual employee, it is different." He said he was unable to give me figures on how many certificates of loss of citizenship had been issued. "We have no statistics on how many have lost their citizenship," he said. "I think the figure is quite high but I don't know what it is. You know a naturalized citizen loses his citizenship after five years unless he returns to the U.S., and some are caught by this.* Washington may have some figures on this, we only try here to keep

* This provision, dating from 1940, was rendered unenforceable by a Supreme Court decision on May 18, 1964, which declared unconstitutional a much older statute which canceled the citizenship of naturalized citizens who returned to their native lands and stayed away from the U.S. for

tabs on how many Americans there are in Israel at any given time." Pressed for numbers, he guessed: "I think it might run an average of one a week, some weeks none, some more, especially in summer, when people want to travel, and that's when we pick them up. I would guess that about fifty a year is about right."

In the earlier years, in the 1950s, he said, more Americans used to come in voluntarily to renounce their citizenship. "Since the middle 1950s, I'd say at least 95 percent have opted out according to the procedure, and most of them are careful about their status. But we still do have maybe two or three a year who come in to renounce their citizenship. Such a person has to say: 'I wish to renounce my American citizenship.' He then fills out a form, swears to it, and that's it. The cases we get now are either youngsters, or once in a while some who are working for the government and have to comply with Israeli government security regulations. We try to discourage them, especially in the case of younger people who might regret it later. This is done by one of our consular officers who explains the whole problem and talks it over with them."

The consular official in charge of discouraging would-be Israeli citizens had a sympathetic attitude toward his wayward charges. "Of course I try to dis-

---

three years. The five-year rule, applying to absence abroad in any country, was not directly involved in the particular case, but was assumed to be nullified also by the decision.—*New York Times*, May 19, 1964. This decision was a liberating one for the "senior citizens" in Israel, most of whom could not easily afford a trip back to the United States to safeguard their status. This decision was a forerunner of the broader ruling of May 29, 1967 affecting Congressional power to legislate about citizenship.

courage them," he said, "I would be derelict if I didn't. I think I have talked three or four of them in the past year into pausing or reconsidering their act. But in two or three cases I was not successful. They are usually youngsters and I ask them whether their families know what they are undertaking to do—usually they don't. I ask whether they don't think they ought to write first to their father and mother and talk it over. They would tell me that they believe in the State of Israel, the land of the Jews, that they don't have to feel inferior here. Some of them would insist on their own strong pro-American attitudes, saying Israel and America were both democracies, but that Israel was a Jewish democracy. Those who are strongest and most adamant about this I would say are from strong Zionist families back home, are between nineteen and twenty-four, come from lower-middle-class families, and have had two years or so at college or a university. They are all intelligent. Such a fellow would say that he wanted to participate more directly in Israel. 'I want to serve in the army, I want to make a cleaner break.' But as I say, we only get two or three like this in a year who make this kind of commitment."

The Committed

For the Americans who did become Israeli citizens, the choice was seldom easy but the commitment was always clear. This, after all, was what coming to Israel

was all about: the re-establishment of the Jewish
nation. This is what Zionism was about, to restore
nationhood to the Jews, to end their wanderings, to re-
establish a Jewish land so that Jews could cease at last
to be alien dwellers in the lands of others. The American Jews who came to Israel came, they said, to take
part in this process of re-creation, to *belong* to the
Jewish nation in a way they could not belong elsewhere, not even in America. The first and most elementary act of belonging, then, was to embrace the
new or the re-established Jewish nationality. This, at
least, was the Zionist logic, and the more Zionist the
individual's background, the easier it was for him to
conform to it—for those who had been brought up to
feel that the return to the Land of Israel was the
ultimate goal of their lives, it was, presumably, a natural step. For those who had come to fight for the new
state and then decided to settle in it for the rest of their
lives, it seemed a necessary commitment, an act of faith
which gave consistency to their acts. There are Zionists
and 1948 veterans, to be sure, who have stopped short
of this final act of attachment and allegiance, but I
suspect that they suffer more than most others from the
consequences of their half-acts. The happiest Americans I encountered in Israel, I think it fair to say, were
those who had carried the logic of their commitment to
Israel to the ultimately symbolic point of joining their
fate to its fate, for better or worse, by becoming citizens. They were the most integrated, if not always the

most contented, and although they were swimming against high seas of many troubles of many different kinds, their troubles were not of *this* kind. They were sufficiently at peace with themselves and with their purposes. They were committed.

The great majority of these committed American Israelis are to be found, as I have indicated, on the kibbutzim. They are, in the main, products of the Zionist youth movements in America. Some came just before the creation of the state, many came just afterward and took part in the epic of reclaiming the land, making it flourish again, defending it against attack, and winning it, finally, for their own. Those who shared in the heroic period were marked by it. No matter how brief that hour was for them, it was their finest, and among them there were relatively few whose commitment to Israel was not full and for whom citizenship in the new state was not an automatic act. "We are all Israeli citizens," said one of these veteran kibbutzniks in some surprise at my question. "We don't see this as a problem. It may be different in the city, but here we have to identify completely. We are Israelis. That is what we are." Another younger man said: "I renounced my American citizenship in 1950. I came to the view that you can't have your cake and eat it, you can't be content to be an 'Anglo-Saxon' in Israel."

Perhaps these committed Israelis will be more dramatically represented here not by a product of the

Zionist movement, not by a kibbutznik, but by a much
more typical product of an American middle-class Jewish background who was probably one of the most
"American" Americans I encountered in Israel. He
was an almost stereotypically American go-getting type
who came to Israel to help fight the Arabs in 1948, who
started with nothing and made a remarkable success as
a man of business. I caught him almost literally on the
fly—an hour before he had to run to catch a plane
south—an athletically slender man, still not yet forty,
with a bushy semi-Sabra-style moustache, cropped hair,
a heavy jaw, and a soft-spoken courteous manner. We
talked after he finished some swift dictation and
though the clock marked the need for hurry, his air
was still quite relaxed.

Son of a modestly successful businessman, he had a
year at college where he had an early important experience: "I really read the Bible for the first time and got
stirred up. I started believing in it. I had always
thought that man made God. I began to think it might
be the other way around." In 1945 at age eighteen he
went into the Marines, and was heading for the Pacific
when that war ended. He began to read in the press
about the holocaust in Europe, the illegal immigration, the underground role of the Haganah in the fight
to transform Palestine into Israel. He was shaken when
he found himself unable to explain his own religion to
a group of friends in his Marine outfit, fellows, he said,
who were greatly interested in each other's religion

and who decided through long bull sessions that the road to the good life was "to do something about what one believed in."

"I decided they were right and it was up to me to do something. I was twenty when I got out of the Marines in 1947 and I decided to come to Palestine. My parents tried to stop me, but I came anyway." He saw action in the short Galilee campaign. Then, during a long lull, he went to a kibbutz for two months. "That was enough for me to decide that I don't believe in socialism," he said. "Here the individual loses his freedom of decision and I don't think that's right. What really happens in the kibbutz is that it gets into its own kind of oligarchy of committees and there are always some guys deciding what you should do and where. No one's free. That really wasn't for me." He took part in the last fighting near Gaza, shooting up Egyptian supply trains for about three weeks. "It was a real long time and we were glad when it ended. You're not supposed to be glad if you're a hero, but we were glad.

"I had decided then that this country was for me," he went on. "I decided that to me, as a Jew, Israel was my home. It seemed to me quite incidental where I or anybody else came from at that moment. I had come across a saying of the rabbis to the effect that a man is made up of soil and the soil that makes him is part of the whole earth, that we each have in us more or less the soil of every place. It seems to me that all Jews have some part of the soil of Israel in them and have just been wandering around in other places for a long while. This is what I believe, anyway."

He returned for another year at college and then a year at Yeshiva University where he studied Hebrew and Jewish history—"There were things I felt I had to know." At this same time he decided to equip himself to be a surveyor in order to start a new life in a new country, and this he duly did, going to night school and a summer field course run by City College of New York. It was this set of skills that led him directly to his later success as an entrepreneur in Israel, but let me here pick up only that further thread of his story that has to do with his becoming an Israeli:

"I gave up my citizenship. I renounced it in 1952, right after I came back. I walked up and down for fifteen minutes in front of the consulate in Haifa before I finally decided to walk in and take the step. It was a lot to think about. After all it was a change, a real change. I was still very much an American. I had been born and brought up there, my parents were there. I suppose it is something like deciding to get married—you hesitate and think twice: maybe I oughtn't to do this. And this is what I was doing that day in Haifa when I walked up and down in front of the consulate. But I now believed there was a place for me to be. And if this was a privilege and a command, if this was fulfilling a divine and a personal destiny, joining myself to all my forefathers, then by God, I thought, I really had to go for it all the way and become a citizen.

If you're going to belong here, I said to myself, then you really go for it all the way and you become a citizen. If you're going to belong here, then you want to be in the army, you want to be part of everything that's going on. If you were in America, you would become an American citizen—that's what all the immigrants did when they came there. I went in.

"You know, I knew evangelists from my days in the Marines; we used to go to missions to get fed when our money would give out on leaves, and we used to sit and listen to them talk, hear them calling the people back to Christ, talk about the great transformation that came over you when you finally came to that moment of accepting Christ. I thought of that when I walked out of that consulate that day. I felt transformed, I felt exhilarated by the step I had taken. I have no regrets."

This kind of starry exultation was easier to come by in the early days, many said, than now, and was largely confined to the young people who came to join the kibbutz movement as pioneers in Israel. Now, one heard on all sides, the kibbutz-type Zionist idealism is ebbing away. The accent has shifted to industrialization, to something called "normalization"—which means something very different from the communal-socialist-utopian dreams that the kibbutzniks had of the good new life in the land of the Jews. The kibbutzim themselves are changing, their place in the

economy shifting, and the old communal austerity giving way, whether slowly or swiftly, to the needs and
demands of greater individual well-being. American
recruits are hard to come by nowadays, and they come
most often not with stars in their eyes but questions in
their minds, questions not easily or readily answered
by what they hear from their age peers on the kibbutz,
the youthful Sabras. I caught only fleeting intimations
of all this as I journeyed by and have no basis for
enlarging upon it. But it is a fact that no great stream
of replacements and reinforcements flows from America now into these little communes and very few of
those who do come make that additional small journey of renunciation to the nearest American consulate.
Among those who come to Israel not to work in the
kibbutzim but to find their places in the cities, tentativeness and caution are much more in evidence.

Those Americans I met who had become Israeli
citizens in more recent years all seemed to have come
to the decision only after a long time and under heavy
pressure, usually connected with their positions in the
government. They spoke of the move not with exhila-
ration but with a certain pain and with their hesitation
still apparent. One was a well-known professional
whose gifts had led him to be selected to represent
Israel at a number of international conferences. His
equivocal status in this role evidently caused him great
discomfort and also brought him under severe pressure
from the Israeli government and his professional col-

leagues. A quiet man with a soft and deliberate manner, he chose not to go into any of the details. He even said he could not remember exactly what year it was that he had given up his American citizenship. He looked out the window across a view of busy construction, the dust and bustle of building construction—a common sight in bustling Israel—and after a long pause he said: "It's a problem, living in such a small society. I can't really say what I feel is lacking. It's a new feeling, just an irritant, I suppose, a minor irritant." When I asked him a little later why Americans generally were reluctant to become Israeli citizens, he gave as his first general reason: "It's a problem, giving up citizenship in a really big country."

Another American I met, an important government servant, had also taken the step a few years before. He began talking about it calmly enough, but as he went on, it became clear the anguish of his decision was still very much with him. "What does one gain by becoming an Israeli?" he asked. "You can vote, you can serve in the army. For me, neither of these things was ever part of the demands of Zionist ideology. As a matter of fact, this is a new thought, citizenship is really an alien concept in Judaism." He went on into a lengthy argument, with citations from the Bible, about how Jews of old regarded their relationship to the state. He then said: "If I come to Israel, I am not repudiating America. But if I give up my American citizenship, then I *am* repudiating America, and this is

not the way I feel. *Why should one have to choose?"*
He paused to collect himself. I murmured that migration was a kind of choice. "Yes," he said, "migration is
a choice, but it is not an act of repudiation—why, there
are a million Americans living abroad now!—but the
act of citizenship makes it formal and legal. Where is
that definite point where an American Jew who comes
to Israel can really say, 'Here, here is where *I cut
myself off!'?"*

The Noncommitted

The great majority of Americans in Israel have not
cut themselves off, and for a great many of them, of
course, this is not an agonizing matter at all.

There are first the old folks, the "senior residents"
who have come to Israel from America to live out their
last years in the promised land on their American
Social Security checks. There are, as indicated earlier,
at least 1,000 of them, perhaps as many as 1,500. They
are almost all foreign-born Americans. Most of them
came to America from Eastern Europe forty or fifty
years ago or more; some smaller number came as refugees just before the Second World War. Most of them,
it appeared, had remained modest working people all
their lives, had only limited formal education, were
more literate in Yiddish than in English, and quite a
few were in Israel as retired beneficiaries of various
Zionist or other Jewish labor or fraternal group pro-

grams for retirement security, and lived in homes maintained by these organizations. A few received monthly checks for as little as $40, others for as much as $150. Most typically, according to several individuals who were much in contact with them, they feel deeply and often very sentimentally grateful to the country which had given them asylum, dignified work, a chance to raise and educate their families, and now made it possible for them to enjoy this degree of personal independence in their late years.

I did not interview any of these older individuals directly, but I did sit for part of a morning next to an enormously kind and devoted young man who was helping them—he was one of those displaced American rabbis who had to hunt out non-rabbinical functions to perform in Israel—by spending part of every day patiently filling out forms for them, answering their questions about a great host of legal or personal problems and trying to direct them to whatever more organized and more official help was available. They cling strongly to their American citizenship, he told me, partly out of the fear—quite unfounded in fact—that if they ceased to be American citizens they would cease receiving their benefits, but also out of a genuine sense of attachment to the land that had done so well by them. There was another feeling too, he thought. He quoted one old woman: "I was already an immigrant once. I don't want to be an immigrant again." Becoming American citizens had been one of the greatest and proudest achievements of their lives and they were not going to yield it now, not even to become Israelis, and anyway, they were Yiddish-speaking Jews and it was too late for them to start trying to become Hebrew-speaking Israelis.

Another morning I sat for an hour listening in on the meeting of the Senior Residents Committee of the AACI convention. It was an arresting experience to come from the other sessions where, whatever else there was, there was also youth and energy, to this roomful of old men and women who were not thinking about the nature of their commitment to America or to Israel but about something they felt to be much closer to each one of them. Their chairman began by naming those who had died during the past year. He complained that the Association had paid neither heed nor honor to the dead. "I told them," the chairman said, "I told them they were all young, but I told them, just wait, someday you'll be old too!" He asked the group to stand for a minute's prayer for those who were gone. The next item of business was about burial plots, the scarcity of burial plots they could afford. As I looked around me, I wondered how these aging men and women passed their days, how they related to each other and to the people around them, and, most of all, I wondered what was the quality of their separation from their children back home in America. But whatever they might have been suffering agony over, if over anything, it was clearly not over the dilemmas of "Jew-ishness" or of being "American" or becoming "Israeli."

A next large number for whom the issue is less pressing, certainly much less immediate, are the new-comers. If in the early days some American immigrants on arrival dropped to kiss the Land of Israel and claim it for their own, there seemed to be few or none such now. Even the smaller numbers of young recruits com-ing to the kibbutzim from the Zionist youth organiza-tions were coming now in a spirit not of high exalta-tion but of high tentativeness: "Give us three years and then we'll see," they were quoted as generally saying. But the greater number of American newcomers to Israel do not come as Zionist recruits and they do not come to the relative certainties of kibbutz existence. They come therefore with much greater uncertainty and greater reason to wonder, on purely material grounds of jobs, housing, language, schooling for their children, whether they are going to be able to "make it." They come strongly briefed about the procedure for not falling inadvertently into the status of "olim" and for remaining "temporary residents" and retain-ing their status as Americans while they find out what kind of life they are going to be able to make for themselves in the Jewish state.

One of the newest newcomers I met was a profes-sional man who after nearly a year of looking had not yet found a place that he felt would satisfy him. "Unless I find a place, I won't stay," he said. "I don't know that I am attached enough to Israel to become a taxi driver in order to stay. I don't know how far I would be willing to go. I am not in the position of the German intellectuals who came here and had no choice, who had no chance to work in their professions and simply had to do something else in order to live. I still have a large area of choice. . . ." He went on:

"They say you have to do what you can and get along but most people don't say this any more. The old Zionist ideology is passé. You don't speak of making sacrifices in coming to Israel. . . . We are middle-class American Jews who need to find a place where we can fit, we are not people who are going to find our satisfactions from physical labor as the old Zionist idealists could. . . . I'm strongly enough attached and identified to want to root myself here, but not that much. Being here is not the be-all or end-all, no. I am not here as a negation of America. I don't negate America or the Diaspora. I am here on a personal basis, not as part of a movement. And there's the problem of dual identification, of getting into a position where you do not have enough of either side. You get to feel that democracy is not deeply rooted here, whether for Europeans or Americans or whomever. I don't have the answers, and I don't know whether I'll stay or not stay."

Becoming an Israeli citizen was not even in his mind

as one of his future possibilities. "That's all right for those who are ready to make the sacrifice," he said. "That would be the most extreme manifestation of uprooting oneself. The largest number of Americans here are not doing that. They are people who are living more or less ambiguously between two worlds. Maybe it will be different with their children, but I feel that they feel more out of the center in Israel than they were in America, and in America they didn't really feel 'out.' Here they are a small minority. I realize this is the truth of the situation but here I am easing myself into it just the same."

Another much more recent newcomer felt differently; he could foresee that he might feel the need of making an eventual commitment to life in Israel. Just now he was having a particularly hard time getting settled, learning the language, beginning to make his living. He thought the question of citizenship was hardly one he could worry about now. Then he went on:

"Frankly, though I can envisage myself getting into political discussions with Israelis, and somebody saying to me: 'Look, you keep your mouth shut. Where do you come in to talk about these things?' I intend to hold on to my American passport. It's too good a thing to give up. America has been good to me, and for the workingman it's the finest country in the whole world. But there may come a time, if everything goes as planned when I'll really be established here, really be adjusted. Then I'll have to make this decision. Am I going to have all the disadvantages without the advantages? I mean the taxes, which are murderously high, and all those problems, the cost of living and so on. But I'll have to ask myself whether I don't want to get into this thing. There's great room for improvement here. Everything is so new. We can all hope to get improvements. . . . I have no Zionist background so it's harder for me. If I were a Zionist, it would be easier because I would be much more tied to begin with, ideologically and so on. It would be easier. But in the end it depends on what you want out of life. I'll have to decide."

There is another kind of person, not a newcomer at all but a long-established resident in Israel, who in quite another way remains quite untroubled by the whole question. I do not know how common a type he might be but the one I met was a well-fixed business-man who had come to Israel many years before—the same one for whom life in Israel made it easier to live, he felt, as an Orthodox Jew. He took a cool view, however, of most of the problems that so greatly agitated most of the other people I met. What bothered him were the business regulations, tax headaches, the difficulty of dealing with the bureaucracy, and the strain of matching wits with European-Israeli competitors. As for the problem of citizenship, he shrugged it off.

"That doesn't bother me at all," he said. "The government is lenient about military service. It has exempted all Americans. You register as an American and you get your exemption automatically. I am here as a permanent resident. This does not bother me at all. The people who are worried about citizenship are the idealists, and the people who worry about ideology, on the one hand, and the people who worry about rights and benefits on the other. I'm not worried about either. It is true you have to be a citizen to participate in political life, but I don't know if my vote would change any of the things here which may not be as I would like them to be."

This brings us, then, to the remaining segment of this small universe of Americans in Israel, the idealists, the ideologists, the people who "worry about rights and benefits" and who therefore worry about the problem of citizenship. It would be difficult, as always in Israel, to know what their numbers might be. It is possible, however, to make a calculated guess. If we use that basic figure of "about 10,000" for the grand total, we can begin by subtracting the 10 percent who have become Israeli citizens and don't have the problem, at least not in this form; I would have no idea at all what percentage to suggest for those who have definitely made the opposite decision, *not* to become Israelis, and having settled this question in their minds have fully rationalized it so that it no longer troubles them. There must be a fair number of people in this category, but there is no peg on which to hang even a guess as to how many there are. We can, however, go on to subtract another 10 percent for the senior citizens. Then the annual arrival and departure figures suggest that we can probably classify about a third of the total as newcomers who are still testing the ground to see if it can hold them and can therefore quite reasonably put off both the external and internal pressures to make this ultimate commitment to it. We come, then, to a guess that we have in view here about half of the total population of American Jews in Israel. These are people who have been living in Israel long enough to get as "settled" or as "adjusted" as they are ever going to be. They have had ample time to face the decision on citizenship and to come to some conclusion about it. Some have concluded not to come to any decision at all. Some keep trying to push the question out of sight. Some have contented themselves with some half-answers with which they manage to live even though they do not half-solve their problems of identity. The shapes of adaptation are endless, and from my brief exploratory encounters with these individuals I certainly do not offer any final word about how any of them have struck their balances. But if not a final word, I do offer a first word; enough, I believe, to suggest some of the range and variety of their responses to their dilemmas as I came upon them, enough to suggest at least an initial outline of how some of these American Jews in Israel describe their condition of semi-commitment.

The Semi-Committed

I asked every American I interviewed in Israel about the problem of citizenship, how he explained his own choice, how he described his own situation. From those who had chosen to remain American citizens, the answers soon became familiarly recurring and began to group themselves in identifiable clusters. To remain an American citizen in Israel was *unimportant*, it was *convenient*, it was a matter of *security*, it was a *tie back* to home, family, country.

> *Unimportance:*
> —*"It's unimportant."*
> —*"A mere formality."*
> —*"Just a technicality."*
> —*"How psychologically important it is to be a citizen?"*
> —*"More of a fuss is made over citizenship than it warrants."*

Early in my inquiry, I sought out one well-known American who, on hearing the purpose of my call, flatly refused to be interviewed about his own experience as an American in Israel. He could not see, he said, that anyone's autobiography was a fit subject for social science research. He said he was willing to talk about the subject in general terms, but when I soon mentioned the general subject of citizenship he reacted as though he had been touched with a live wire. He sat up suddenly straight and waved my question off with an almost panicky insistence: "Just a sheer formality!" he said sharply. "A mere formality, nothing of any importance whatever!" I mildly observed that I had met other Americans in Jerusalem who had seemed to think it was quite important. With a glassy, closed smile, he ignored my remark. Our conversation ended briefly thereafter. A few days later, in another interview, a friend of this individual described him as "a man having a love affair with Israel" and, without any ironic or sarcastic intent, volunteered the information that he had been living in Israel for twelve years and had never become an Israeli citizen.

This was an extreme case. No one else I met during my whole time of question-asking in Israel refused outright to try to answer my questions. But I did interview quite a few who thought, as this man said he did, that the "problem of passports" was "unimportant" or "purely technical." Usually in response to further questions, they did their best to explain their view to me and, often it seemed, to themselves. One person, for example, said he did not think it was "psychologically important" to be a citizen. He had settled, he said, for his own marginality. Although he expected to live for the rest of his life in Israel, he held on to his American passport, he said, purely as a matter of convenience.

> *Convenience:*
> —"*It's easier to travel on an American passport.*"
> —"*The important thing is the ease of moving back and forth.*"
> —"*You don't have to stand in line or fill out papers at the consulate.*"
> —"*There's the family back home, responsibilities, emergencies, you might want to get back there in a hurry. If you're an Israeli, you have to wait weeks for an American visa.*"
> —"*If you have to travel for business reasons, it's much more convenient to be an American.*"

The claim of convenience was by far the most commonly offered. It was part of nearly every reply that was made. Each person had his own variation of the theme and each one his own measure of reality in his answer.

"I came in 1950," said a well-established dweller in Jerusalem. "I met people who in the enthusiasm of the fighting or in the Messianic spirit of the time had become Israeli citizens. But then they had awful trouble getting a visa to go back to the United States. It would take six weeks sometimes, all kinds of red tape. I was advised, don't give it up, it's convenient. So I held on." He went on: "I am careful not to vote, and I fill out a slip each year to be released from military service." And then he added: "I know I can't go on indefinitely this way, I know." But he had been going on this way for thirteen years, and is still.

Actually I heard many conflicting versions of just how difficult it was for an Israeli citizen to travel to the United States. Every person who said it was difficult was either an American citizen or one of that small number who have managed to retain an unofficially dual status. Their versions ranged from complaints about Israelis having to stand on line at the consulate, to having to wait for weeks, and on up to waiting for "a year and a half" while some darkly McCarthyist political cloud was dispersed. But when I checked these stories with Americans who had become Israeli citizens, the difficulties shrank or evaporated altogether. "My own experience," said one veteran citizen-settler in a fairly typical response, "was that it took me less time to get a visa on my Israeli passport than it took some Americans I know to get their papers in order for a return home."

The strongest versions of difficulties in travel came from those who were identifiably "leftist" in their local political affiliations, and from several of these individuals I gathered that the "convenience" of the

American passport was very largely political. Thus at a certain kibbutz one night, an American kibbutznik who had been in Israel more than ten years had just finished explaining to me that keeping one's American passport was a convenient thing for going to see one's parents, when a neighbor put his head in the door. "Your mother left her umbrella here when she was here," the visitor said. There was some talk about how to get the umbrella back to his mother. When the visitor left, I asked: "So your parents are here?" "Oh yes," he said, "they live in Haifa." He did not say it sheepishly, although he clearly had not intended to mention this small fact in connection with the convenience of keeping his American passport. This was a kibbutz that belonged to the left-wing segment of the kibbutz movement. Unlike the social democratic Habonim kibbutzniks, these were people who took a looser or more "pragmatic" view of issues of this kind. "In the early days," one of them explained to me, "we thought the passport was a symbol of a tie with the past, something to be done away with. But this was a youthful idea. After a while, as mature persons, we found that this symbolic thing made no difference. If you wanted to give up and go back, you went back. It wasn't the passport that made the difference. We were interested in having it easy for people to go back, whether for the movement or to see their parents." He grinned unpleasantly. "You see, the American authorities have certain attitudes toward certain political

parties. Toward the Mapam, to which most of us belong, they are downright antagonistic. One of our
members was held up for a year and a half for a visa
when he wanted to go see his sick mother. So we solve
the problems of military service and voting. We try not
to compromise ourselves and we also try to fulfill *all*
our obligations."

An ex-member of this group told me: "The movement ordered certain people to keep their passports for
future travel in order to go back and forth more easily
on the business of the movement. This applied to those
leadership types, the youth movement types, not necessarily the best types." Later at another older kibbutz
belonging to this same political persuasion, I met some
of its better "types," older people who had evidently
held on to that naïve "youthful idea" and had taken a
strong, even a puritanical stand on the necessity to
adopt citizenship.

Security:
   —*"It's like an insurance policy."*
   —*"Who knows how things will work out?"*
   —*"For the road back . . ."*
   —*"Just in case . . ."*
   —*"It's the kind of trump card you don't give up*
     easily."
   —*"It's nice to be the ward of a big strong country."*
   —*"It's a matter of not burning bridges."*

These answers seemed to come closer to reality, closer to that opaque zone of the truth in which it is so hard to find one's way. Coming to Israel had to be an act of faith, on both personal and broader grounds. The immediate difficulties were formidable, the risks numerous, and the future highly uncertain. Faith had limits. The fact that Americans have "a place to go back to" would be translated by some Israelis as meaning that Americans had a place to run to when the going got rough. To this some Americans would retort that these Israelis were not more committed to remaining in Israel, just envious of the Americans' ability to leave. At the time of the Suez crisis in 1956 when the American authorities advised all Americans to leave the area, only about fifty residents (as distinct from tourists), I was told, packed up and took off. This fact, of course, has since been used on both sides of the argument. Americans cite it to show how few of them ran in face of danger; their critics use the fact that some Americans *did* run to support their more sweeping charges. A European Israeli official whose job kept him in close touch with Americans brushed such charges away as unworthy and untrue. "I don't think Americans are afraid of an Arab attack. It is not for this that they need to keep a gate open, a door to go back through. I think in their hearts they want to stay, they want to live here, and thousands of them have stayed, many for more than ten years. But it's a new country, a poor country, and a person can fail to be able to live here. I think this is what they feel, this is why they want to be able to go back in case they have to. . . ."

Among the long-established American residents I met in Israel, very few, I should guess, seriously thought of America as a haven from some future Arab attack in Israel. Their fears and uncertainties were much more complex than that. I met only one individual myself, a woman, who admitted that she remained an American citizen because she might want to run when the bombs began to fall. She was the wife of a successful businessman and described herself as being very Orthodox. Indeed, she said, only the most ultra-Orthodox sects in Israel were truly, truly Jewish, and it was only her own frailty of flesh and spirit that kept her from joining them. I listened for a long time to the story of her devotion to Israel and also her husband's. It then developed that her son had reached age eighteen the year before the Sinai campaign. She wriggled quite hard for quite a while before acknowledging that yes, he had chosen at that time to get out of military service by retaining his American citizenship. Her daughter was not obliged to serve, she went on with bright relief, because she was Religious and was exempt on that count. She told me her husband was an important man, and that it was important, for Israel's sake, for him to keep his American passport so that he could easily travel to many places and do useful things for Israel. "It's a kind of trump card that you don't give up so easily," she said, "not only for oneself but for Israel." There was a pause and then suddenly she burst out: "Well, maybe deep down I don't really want to give it up. Maybe I've just found some kind of rationalization." And what, I asked, did she think was "deep down" there? "Well," she said, "I could make a speech about American patriotism in answer to this. I was terribly American, my grandmother was American. I couldn't really have lived in any other place besides America except in Israel." Did she plan to spend the rest of her life in Israel? She said she did. Then why not become a citizen of Israel? She answered agitatedly, "Because Jews are threatened, Jews are always threatened, and this is a kind of ace in the hole. Yes, I suppose it *is* a weakening. That's the trouble with us Americans, we *do* have a place to go back to— you know some people left at the time of Sinai. How long would *I* stick it out if the Egyptians start throwing rockets?" I said I didn't know, how long did she think? "I don't know," she flung back at me, "I don't know. But there it is, always there, a subtle factor in back of everything."

She reverted to religion, then, and lectured me for half an hour on the theme that the important thing, after all, was not physical survival but spiritual survival, and she thought this was even more threatened in Israel by the secular and the godless Jews. She knew what was "right," she said, but she didn't have the moral courage to be "right" herself; the Naturei Karta —the most ultra of the ultrareligious sects which refused to recognize the State of Israel—was "right," she said, but she wasn't "right" enough herself to join them. "What's 'right' anyway?" she demanded to know. "It's right if a man pays absolutely 100 percent on his income tax, every penny. *That's* being *right*— but who does that? Who is *that* right? The same with me, I'm no angel." I said I could see that. She moved into a lengthy argument in support of Jewish Orthodoxy against all forms of revision or change. I edged out of the door murmuring something about other appointments. She followed me out onto the landing still talking, and her voice followed me down the stairs, and then I was outside, and the stiflingly hot air of the sun-bright Tel Aviv street felt cool on me as I walked rapidly away.

There were no doubt others like this woman among the semi-committed American Jews in Israel but I was fortunate in not meeting them. Among most of those I did meet, the issue was more complicated. They were people who spoke about "not burning bridges" and while this had some element of their own personal security in it, they were talking about bridges back to something much more than safety. They were talking about holding on to what tied them to their American origins, a tie they could not bring themselves to cut.

The Tie:
  —*"It's an emotional thing, it's part of you. . . ."*
  —*"America did nothing to cause me to cut myself off from it."*

—*"I guess we want to eat our cake and have it too."*

—*"I promised my mother I wouldn't cut off my tie with home. . . ."*

—*"Wanting the tie back is part of it . . .* it's *there."*

—*"Before, my wife used to say it was because she might want to get home quickly, her father was ill. But then her father died, and since then this has hardened into a kind of shrine."*

—*"One's citizenship is a symbol of identity. . . ."*

—*"We are the desert generation."*

Here among these answers we come upon the greater obscurity and painful confusion of behavior and goals. These are the individuals whose motivations are the most mixed, whose behavior is the most contradictory, and whose agony over all this is, therefore, the greatest and the most private. Almost all of those quoted are individuals deeply and devotedly engaged in the tasks they have taken on in Israel and they have all stuck it out for many years. One is a woman who has lived for more than a decade on a kibbutz, borne her children there, gone from one scrubby work-task to another doing "women's work" in the larger "home" of the kibbutz instead of "woman's work" in the smaller home that was her own. She was left with a great sense of weariness and a great need to convince herself that it all had been the right thing to do. Now her parents had come to join her and her brother, also a member of the same kibbutz, and their families, and she had only now, finally, "initiated procedure to become an Israeli citizen." She said she did not know what her brother and his wife, also still American citizens, were doing about it. "I mentioned it to him," she said, "but he hasn't answered me and I just haven't gone into it." She now felt at last that she was in Israel to stay forever and might just as well take the final step after all these years; but she still could not discuss this fundamental decision with her fellow-kibbutznik brother.

Many of the shapes of this most painful ambivalence show through the words of a government servant who had been working devotedly and single-mindedly for the state since just after it was created. Here is some of what he said:

"Israel is a special kind of state with some unbelievable aspects, for example the open door to all Jews, and I don't think it can be narrowly nationalist, I don't think it needs this citizenship rule, that government officials should be citizens of the state. It is very difficult in the modern world to take on such a thing unconditionally. I think the number of those who come here and kiss this soil and tear up their passports is zero. We all have conditional ideas. How can one be absolutely nationalist?

"It is true that if you want to live the good life you have to commit yourself to something, and to the extent that Americans do not do this, they create a lot of anxiety for themselves here. Some do commit themselves all the way and a lot of this burden falls off. The others always have the road back. I have read Martin Buber on how hard it is for a person to commit himself. I know. I'm not committed, I don't say I am. But I have to find a way of commitment. Most men find this hard in their lives. Belongingness is a key thing. I have found a great yearning for belongingness in O'Neill and in the Greeks and in Shakespeare. I think that where there is commitment you get nobility. I have to find the meaning of my own commitment.

"And the question of citizenship gets all wrapped up in this. The physical act of taking up life here is a big commitment in itself. Coming here is the most important part of it. But wanting that tie that is back of you is part of it. It's there. It's part of the non-commitment that is also involved.

"Is it then really something short of actually belonging?" he demanded to know. "Americans have their values and their ties to the American system and milieu and can't shake them off. If I spelled out all my values and how I would want this country to be run, it would not be too far from the Anglo-Saxon model, the concept of life, government, human relations. People say to me that I'm as American as anybody who has just arrived. I don't think this is uniquely American. I think it happens to everybody who comes here. You can't shake off your past. All people hold on to their old values—and this is what makes me part of the desert generation. But the American values in politics and in the social sense are extremely important. Every American feels this, even those who live in the kibbutzim, in that attempt at an Essene society—everybody tries to go by Anglo-Saxon rules. Every American wants more development of freedom here, everybody's pack of agonies, everybody's pack of troubles, is mixed up with both personal things and these large things."

He began to identify what he thought needed to be changed, the things that needed "Anglo-Saxon" answers. "In 1950 there seemed to be more sense of destiny and direction than there is today. I think the sense of belonging is tied up in this—an American needs this compensation for what he does here, I know that. But all this was much less clear in 1950. Everything here now bothers me. The school situation is a mess. The politics is a mess, there is something terribly wrong with the political framework of life here. There is no force pulling in a consistent direction, everything is a deal. Oh, I don't know. This is all so very difficult to try to say and to explain . . ." He stopped, and then he said: "Maybe it's simply that I'm just getting older." He went on to speak for a long time of his work, which was connected with key areas of the development of the country's economy and his grasp of facts sounded encyclopedic, his range total, his engrossment complete, and his frustration great but not fatal. After he had finished describing his failure to win support for a particular policy or project which he thought crucially important, he said: "You just keep plugging away at it. You've got to have faith it will come out somehow." He smiled a bit ruefully at himself. "You know," he said, "there could be someone who keeps his passport as an insurance policy and yet is really more committed than someone who gives up his passport and then regrets it." He came back to the ultimate consoling thought I heard from many individuals in this position: "Maybe it will be a matter of time, time and children. The Germans who came here in 1935 in the first wave out of Germany were very outsiderish. Now their children are grown up and they have become quite a powerful element in the country and in business. Maybe it will be that way with us."

The theme of the children was an ever-recurring theme among these individuals. *They* would not quite make it, but their children would. It was their solace and their hope and their ultimate answer to all their riddles. For those whose children are still young, it remains a way of letting the riddles wait.* Some of

* In his "Pangs of Aliyah," loc. cit., Sholom Kahn prints a little poem he wrote in 1955 after his daughter was born:
As I sat in Jerusalem, in the heat of the day,
dream of ruins rebuilt and flowering fields,
I remembered New York, the Bronx, and the City Center
and ice cream parlor Specials in the evenings.
As I sat on the rocks in the beautiful ruins,
remembering Broadway, Morningside, Bryant Park,
a voice within me wept: Ah, when will my City
be one with my Dream and the memories of my years?
Then an angel came, in the heat of the day and whispered:
Behold, a child shall be born whose name shall be Laughter,

those whose children are growing up are going through the trying experience of seeing a gulf open up between them. "There's a cultural gap between my daughter and myself," said one father. "My books are in English, my culture is American. I read *Time*. My horizons are broader. But my daughter is an Israeli. She reads Hebrew. I can't talk with her about a good Hebrew novel or a bad Hebrew novel. She's in the Hebrew culture as we are not. I'm sorry I can't share these experiences with her. My wife is better rooted in Hebrew. But my daughter can talk these things over much better with her house nurse who is a Sabra."

Another father, who has been in Israel for years but has never mastered Hebrew or become an Israeli citizen, also spoke of the gap created by language: "I know now how my father must have felt when we were kids in Brooklyn, and I guess how my kids must feel, the same way I felt. I know how ashamed I used to feel when I heard my old man speak his broken English, and I really made sure that my English wouldn't sound like that [his English was actually pure Brooklyn]. But here I am now in the same position with my kids. I wonder how they feel when they hear me speak my broken Hebrew, and it's all turned around because they're the ones that speak English with an accent."

This father was one of the many who had never

---

and you shall strengthen her bones and she shall repay you.
In the heat of the day, she shall play on these rocks, and flourish,
and the real shall be dream, and your fields in truth shall flower,
in the shade and peace, here, eating the fruit of your fig tree.

found it possible to give up his American citizenship because he could not bear to "burn bridges" to that past life and he kept secretly thinking that one day he would go back. It bothered him to think that his pretty teen-age daughter would never know the pleasures and opportunities of a young woman in America—she had just chosen under characteristic kibbutz pressure not to try to go to the university and he made no secret of how unhappy this made him—and his son, a moustachioed young kibbutznik, had already done his military service and was embarked on his own life committed forever to Israel. But this family, knit by great loving warmth, lent support to the common hope that the children would solve what their parents left unsolved. The son, who had been through the difficult experience of growing up in a tight little community where his parents' nonconforming pattern was looked upon very much askance, was solid in his affection. "My parents held on to their citizenship because they planned to go back to visit. . . . This didn't bother me. At one time maybe it was one way of not burning their bridges. But now they're really settled here. There is nothing really for them to go back to, so it's out of the picture, completely." He grinned. "We, the kids," he said, "we burn the bridges for them."

But when it came to choosing metaphors, most of these non-Israeli Americans much preferred to think of themselves, not as nonburners of bridges but as wanderers in the desert, modern heirs of the Jews who wandered for forty years in the wilderness on their way from Egypt to the Promised Land. I heard it again and again: "We are the desert generation, doomed to wander, never to arrive." Between them and a full commitment to Israel, they saw a wide space they never expected to cross. But from the other side, looking back, were those Americans who *had* become Israeli citizens, and all they saw was a narrow little space, a single step, a single decision away.

The Uncrossed Desert

Between Americans who had become Israelis and Americans who had not lay not a desert but a zone of a certain careful silence, a delicate line down its center, with restrained judgments on the one side and something between discomfort and shame on the other. The judgments of the American Israelis on their fellow-American non-Israelis were—as they were expressed to me—sometimes harsh, sometimes sorrowful, sometimes both. Most of the citizens I met seemed to remember their own private agony before they resolved the issue for themselves. They remained charitable toward those who have not done so. Indeed, in more than one instance, a citizen who wanted to judge noncitizens would also have to judge his noncitizen wife.

"All Americans here have a great ambivalence about this," explained one of the most thoughtful and most devoted American Israelis I encountered during my inquiry. "No one really came here who didn't like America. We want to have the best of two worlds and have to decide where our prior loyalties lie. I myself came out of the Zionist labor movement, I came here in 1949, and it was three years before I decided to give up my citizenship and become an Israeli citizen. It was not an easy thing to do. I was very apprehensive about it. Why give up such a valuable thing, perhaps the most valuable thing in the world? I spent many days and nights thinking and worrying about it before I finally took the step."

Often quoted in this spirit is the testimony of Moshe Kerem, formerly Murray Weingarten, who helped found the kibbutz Gesher-Haziv. He wrote in his book *Life in a Kibbutz:**

I live [in Israel] by choice, not from compulsion. Since I am a native American, Israel does not represent an escape from an "intolerable" way of life. I have faith in American political and social development, and I have no fears about my ability to take my place in American society. It is because I find kibbutz life in Israel a challenging, interesting, and personally satisfying experience that I live there, not because I have a negative attitude towards America or American Jewish life.

*New York, 1955.

Or here again, from another citizen:

"You come here wanting to be a hero, but it's not easy to want to be a hero to the extent of giving up your citizenship. These people are not running away from America. America is still good for them. Their families are still in America. They are not anti-American. In fact, the American who comes here gets more and more pro-American."

I encountered at least one citizen who did not temper his view of noncitizens with any such charity. This was at a lunch I had one day with two government officials, one a veteran American settler who had become an Israeli and one who was also a veteran in Israel but had remained an American citizen. The lunchtime talk had opened a wide difference between the two, the first tending to put all his answers to questions in terms that minimized difficulties, and the other insisting on a hardheaded, realistic view. When the noncitizen left, the citizen visibly relaxed. He explained that the fellow who had just left "had to be realistic" because of the demands of his particular job—"but," he added, "Israel has been built not out of realism but out of impossibilities." A moment or two later he mentioned that the departed guest was not a citizen and he spoke bluntly: "I condemn him for not becoming an Israeli citizen. I condemn my own sister for this too!"

Others spoke more softly. Said one citizen-veteran:

"I made a speech earlier this year in which I told a

group of Americans that I thought there was no real integration unless one took on Israeli citizenship, otherwise one had only one foot in. Many of them objected to my saying this. . . . I can remember that as a child in America I wanted my immigrant parents to become American citizens. The same holds here now. Those who feel more deeply about Israel are more convinced, are here for better or worse—they become citizens. Maybe this is not fair to the others, but I am afraid I think the noncitizen a less moral person, less ethical. He wants the best of two worlds. This may be a more convenient position to hold, but it is a less ethical one. In my opinion this becomes a main issue for every individual. Here we are surrounded by enemies. What is one going to do if things get into crisis, run away? How do you explain a thing like this to your children? Is this really just a matter of convenience? Does it mean you don't really believe in the future of Israel? Another thing, if you're not in politics here, you're right out of the center of affairs. Some Americans say they want to change the electoral system here. How can you even begin to do this is you are not a citizen?"

Again, from a prominent American kibbutznik:

"I don't think anybody can really feel involved and integrated if he hasn't found it possible to choose Israeli citizenship. The American holds on to his citizenship for conscious utilitarian reasons. . . . It is like money in the bank and the individual concerned feels it has nothing to do with the sense of belonging. But I believe it raises an ethical question. He is 'in' the group but with a moral flaw. He is morally a shirker, a flawed individual. I am afraid such people have not really solved the problem of where they belong."

I asked the onetime Marine what he thought about this and he said:

"It is hard to stand in anybody else's shoes. I think they are doing the wrong thing for themselves. It prevents them from doing what they came here today to do, which was to come back home. *This* is our home, our family. A lot of things happen in your family that you don't like, but it's *your* family. If you come to Israel to affirm this, and then you deny it, it puts you in a tough position. I would not want to be one of those people—they are not really good Israelis and they're not really good Americans."

There was, finally, an American who had fought to win the state and had become a citizen when it was created, who said that he felt a wondering unhappy sympathy for those Americans "who came to Israel in search of roots" and then failed to root themselves in the new soil.

"There is tremendous soul-searching in such people. I find it difficult to imagine myself in their skins, but it is also difficult for me to imagine that this is not a deeply serious problem for every one of them, for it comes up all the time, all kinds of burning issues of military service, of politics, of participation. The prob-

lem is always there. They come in a search for whole-
ness but then they don't go the whole way toward it.
This must make them feel a defect in themselves, they
have failed to overcome whatever it is that makes them
act this way. Does a Jew come to Israel just to be an
'expatriate'? The person who does this deprives himself
of the only thing that he really came to Israel to get.
You go to Israel from America because you think you
are just a spectator in America and the role of a spectator is not enough. But then you cut yourself off from
participating. Perhaps this can be understood, but I
am afraid I don't really understand it. The test is:
What are you made of? What makes you tick? Can you
do what you aspire to do?"

I reminded him that most such Americans in Israel
described themselves as members of a "desert generation," wanderers to the Promised Land which not they
but their children would enjoy. He shook his head.
"I'm sorry, I can't buy that," he said. "It's only a
rationalization, a poetic way of saying you don't want
to face the issue. All of us, all of us in Israel are now a
desert generation. Think of the deserts we have to
cross to make Israel really the Promised Land—language, industry, the whole material level, the assimilation of immigrants. There are some of these deserts
that we won't get across easily or quickly, maybe some
we won't be able to cross at all. But the problem of
citizenship is not *this* kind of desert. Talk about the
great bulk of the Moroccans and the others who may

not be able to cross the desert of centuries! *That's* a desert! There are many deserts like *that* in Israel. Deserts between backwardness and modernization, between resources and needs. But the Americans and their problem of citizenship are not on much of a desert. They *can* cross it. All they have to do is go across. Why don't they do it? Perhaps one has to seek irrational rather than rational explanations for this. But believe me, no one really has to wander in *that* little desert if he doesn't want to—all he has to do is cross it."

The American Uniqueness

The small group of American Jews so briefly glimpsed in these pages are caught here at a moment in passage; each one will somehow come or not come to his own destination, his own conclusion, his own sorting out of his mingled identities. Somewhat like Jacob of old, each one is wrestling with a dimly seen opponent, struggling with being *American* and *Jewish* and trying to be *Israeli* without knowing what it means to be any one of the three, much less all three at once. Each of these is an identity in process of fresh formation, each becoming something different from what it was or seemed to be. In this confusion and obscurity, each man's truth is his own; the desert *is* wide and forbidding to him who sees it so; the passage *is* narrow to the one who has found the crossing easier.

Still, without being able to suggest that they apply to any particular individuals, we do have a number of explanations that have been offered for their behavior as a group. Early in these pages I quoted one settler as remarking, only half-facetiously, that since they were so few in number, the reasons for the behavior of Americans in Israel were locked into each one's individual personality and that it was useless to look for any larger design. We were concerned here with only a few thousand from among nearly 6,000,000 American Jews. Each one's self-selection for this particular ordeal by ambivalence no doubt was rooted in the peculiar character of his own self and his own circumstances. I have no doubt this is true or partly true in some cases, but I could hardly testify to any particulars. The testing of this proposition waits on the enterprise of some psychologist and on the making of better keys than we now have for unlocking the secrets of the individual personality or, more promisingly perhaps, on the perceptions of a novelist who may yet appear from among these Americans to tell us what they were like as they wrestled with their dilemmas. The psychologist might be able to locate some of their common idiosyncrasies; the novelist may locate them in their settings. But in the presence of the larger frames of existence in which these individuals are American and Jewish and becoming or trying to become Israeli, it is plain that no matter how critical they may be in any single case, such individual idiosyncrasies cannot be the whole story.

My own proposition is that a larger part of the story has to do with the fact that these Jews are Americans, that there is an American uniqueness which imposes itself on them whether they acknowledge it or not, and that this uniqueness makes their experience different from that of other Jews who are not Americans. Ernest Stock wrote ten years ago: "It may be that at the bottom of the American Jew's vulnerability in Israel . . . there lies the fact that he looks for self-fulfillment as an American no less than as a Jew; whether he knows it or not, his is often a search for commitment within the framework of the American culture."* He was referring mainly to the "early disappointment" of those Americans who had come to Israel and left, but I think his observation applies with no less force to those who have remained. Among those who have done so as fully committed citizens of Israel, there are, as I have shown in several instances, a need and desire to translate their American conceptions of the good life into Jewish and Israeli terms. Among the larger number who have found this full commitment so much more difficult to make, the continuing difficulty lies in closing the gap between their identifications with America and their expectations of Israel.

One common way of describing—and dismissing— this difficulty is to say that it has mainly to do with the gap in material standards of living in the two coun-

* Ernest Stock, "Americans in Israel," *Midstream*, Summer, 1957.

tries. In a 1965 article in *Commentary*,* Ronald Sanders reported that "many Israelis" see American Jews as "spoiled children, irretrievably addicted to the middle class comforts they enjoy in the United States." In Israel, "Europeans and Israelis alike tend to see American civilization as morally weakened by affluence and self-indulgence." Sanders went on to observe that "the irony is that many Americans see themselves in the same way" and indeed are attracted to Israel in the first place because "it seems to offer an alternative to [their] overly comfortable way of life." But this "passion for austerity" does not endure very well, especially since the old Zionist ideal of austerity has been giving way among Israelis generally to their own taste for "affluence and the appetite for comfort." In time, he concluded, "the majority of Americans who remain in Israel therefore end up by striking a balance between the relative luxury they knew back home and the zeal for renunciation which accompanied their original arrival in Israel." It is, of course, a fact that a great many would-be settlers from America have been defeated in Israel by the problems of day-to-day living, whether it was a matter of frustrated romantic self-denial, defeated utopianism, or the simple failure to achieve what they considered to be the needed minimum terms of daily existence. But there is more in American materialism than a passion for creature comforts and more than materialism in the pull of the

* "Settling in Israel?" *Commentary*, August, 1965.

American culture on the American in Israel. He feels
it in his response to everything he finds in Israel, its
politics, its religion, indeed the whole quality of life he
finds there, the prospect of fulfillment it offers him
compared with the choices he can still have at home in
America.

It has been argued that this is far from being a
uniquely American problem in Israel, that many
European Israelis of the present adult generation (and
presumably "Oriental" Israelis as well) also feel the
pull of their former homelands or are governed in
their attitudes and behavior by the cultures in which
they were born, even where these were notably in-
hospitable to Jews. This is a simple truth that has to do
with such things as language, food, often with topog-
raphy, even smells and noises, with the ineradicable
nostalgic attachment to the memories of childhood, the
styles of life which we all carry with us through all our
years. In few places is this more dramatically demon-
strated than in present-day Israel, where the differences among Jews from different cultures are so much
more visible than their similarities. Sometimes this
simple truth is reduced to the simpleminded proposition that today's "wilderness generation," like its biblical predecessor, is merely yearning after Egypt's fleshpots.* But again, there is more to this matter than

* E.g., in a reply to some of my observations as they appeared in maga-
zine form, an English immigrant in Israel, writing in the Jerusalem *Post*
(January 13, 1967), suggested that "a sound survey has to compare
[the Americans] with other national groups of immigrants. In each case,

golden calves, fleshpots, or even childhood memories
or styles of life, more that has to do with Israel itself.
Obviously, all kinds of Israelis, including many born
in Israel, can and undoubtedly do share some of the
troubled concerns and ambivalences felt by some
Americans about the Israeli experience.

This is sometimes focused on a feeling about the
contrast between larger and more cosmopolitan cultures and the smaller "local" or "provincial" situation
of Israel. An Israeli friend of mine, the Sabra son of an
early immigrant from Central Europe, pointed out
that his "cosmopolitan personality" led him to feel
ambivalent toward his own smaller locality and to do
all he could to "hold on to every possible means of
contact and communication with the outside world."
Comparing himself to the Americans in Israel, he went
on: "The only sense in which I am spared the agonies
of indecision is the legal sense [i.e., the choice of
nationality] and whether this makes my position vis-à-
vis the Israeli society any easier to resolve or to handle
than the American's position is to my mind debatable."
In a recent book about Israel, Ronald Sanders identi-

---

the first generation is the generation of the wilderness, looking back to
the fleshpots of Egypt as well as forward to the Promised Land of their
children. The American Jews look back with longing on many aspects of
America. . . . At the same time the Moroccan, Rumanian, and German
Jews looked back with longing to certain aspects of life in Morocco, Rumania, and Germany. . . ." The writer does not specify for the Moroccans
or Rumanians, but the jarred reader learns a few lines further that the
"fleshpots" missed by the German Jew are in "his beer garden," while
the American Jew is yearning "for his corner drugstore . . . the French
Jew for his bistro and the English Jew for his pub."

fied this as a not uncommon state of mind. The "transformation from *European Jew* into Israeli," he wrote,
"was not achieved without a certain accompanying
anxiety [about] turning away from the mainstream of
European civilization to take up a resolutely *provincial*
cultural stance. . . . Nowadays Israelis of European
extraction tend to be troubled by the thought that they
might be living in an extremely provincial cultural
situation."* This is the feeling that the return to
Israel might be not so much a liberation from exile as a
severance from the larger world, even a return to the
Pale in a new form. This anxiety generates other questions that bear heavily on any such individual's view of
the nature and prospects of Israel and his own commitment to it. What will be the character of a new generation of Jewish nationalists, Israelis pouring all their
energies into muscle and pride? What kinds of "Jews"
will tomorrow's Israelis become, and how will they
relate to Jews outside Israel? If Israel is to create a new
kind of "Jew," will it be the kind of Jew such Europeans or Americans will be happy to see their children
become? What are the role and meaning, beyond sheer
self-defense, of a new Jewish nation in a world sick
above all with the harsh narrownesses and other
diseases of nationalism? On what basis can one have
faith that Jewish or Israeli nationalism will be something different from all other nationalisms? All such

* *Israel, the View from Masada*, p. 199.

questions come down at bottom to the question that underpins them all: What is a Jew? It must concern all kinds of Israelis, those most fully committed to the dream of achieving a great rebirth of the Jews through the re-creation of Israel, as well as those who are shaken and made uncertain by what they discover to be some of the realities and limitations of this effort.

Europeans and Americans in Israel can and do share these concerns; but there is a difference between them, and this difference, I believe, is the crux of our present matter. It is the difference between the historic experience of Jews in Europe and in America, between the quality of their identities as "Europeans"—or more particularly as "Englishmen" or "Frenchmen," not to say as "Germans" or "Poles" or "Rumanians"—and as "Americans." The difference lies most crucially of all, I think, in the alternatives that Europe now offers compared with those that beckon from America.

The Europeans in this case are feeling the pulls of an existence they were able to enjoy up to a point as Europeans but much less so—and often not at all—as Jews. When Jews began to acquire European nationalities in the emancipation from the ghetto that followed the French Revolution, it was to no small extent at the cost of their identity as Jews. Indeed, this was often an implicit part of the contract. The liberal Gentiles who pressed for Jewish emancipation saw it as a way for Jews to shed their Jewishness, and there were many Jews ready to accept the invitation to drop the burden of centuries at last. In large numbers they did their best to disappear into the non-Jewish mass. Those Jews who were happy to become citizens of the world outside the ghetto but had no wish to cease being Jews entered into varying degrees of continuing apartness, new patterns of rejection, exclusion, and victimization. This much emancipation never did reach Eastern Europe, and the result there by the end of the nine- teenth century was a mass exodus, most of it to America. The precariousness of the Jew's position, dramatized by the pogroms in the unemancipated East and by the Dreyfus affair in the emancipated West, spurred the rise of political Zionism, the search for a national-territorial solution to the problem of the per- sistent separateness of the Jews among their cosmopoli- tan fellow Europeans. It was out of Germany, finally, where assimilation had gone furthest and cosmopoli- tanism had borne some of its finest fruits, that anti- Semitism reached its ultimate violence. Europe became the graveyard of all but a handful of its Jews; what it could offer the survivors was something less than the beginning of a life of greater promise.

Americans, on the other hand—especially Ameri- cans of the present young adult generation—come out of a society and a national experience which, for all its legacies from Europe, has moved along different paths toward different outcomes, not only for Jews but for all its people. What has marked America off from Europe has been not its size, its productive system, nor

even its great diversity, but rather its creedal commitment to the goal of an open society. The American
experience has been filled over the generations by
virulent bigotry, exclusion, and violence directed at
almost all its religious and racial minorities, its Catholics and Jews, its Chinese and Japanese and Mexicans,
and, most of all, its Negroes. But this has gone on in
constant and gnawing contradiction not merely to the
professed Christianity of its majority—Europe has
been living that way for centuries—but also to the
secular credo of the society. This is what has made for
what has been called the American dilemma. The secular claims that a society makes for itself are far more
subject than its religious professions to the pressure of
social and economic forces that come to bear upon it.
Very large facts, great events, and powerful forces have
moved in largely blind, if not mysterious, ways to
compel some closing of the gap between profession and
practice in America. Its huge size, its great room for
growth, its need for people—all led to the opportunity
it offered to masses of immigrants from so many places.
This led to its development within a century from a
small relatively homogeneous society into a huge
heterogeneous society, with all kinds of groups carving
out and winning their places in it, often—as in the case
of labor, for example—only after long, turbulent, and
sometimes violent conflict. Finally, the great world
crises, wars, and revolutions of this generation have
pushed America harder and harder (often paradoxi-

cally and against the will of a great many Americans)
toward the swifter implementation of its own stated
goals. The events that have transformed white-
nonwhite power relations everywhere in the world
have also forced the long-delayed radical revision of
white-nonwhite relations in the American society. The
threatening rise of totalitarian rivals to American
power has forced the American democracy to become
more democratic, to work harder and faster at elimi-
nating its persisting inequalities and reducing its
margins of poverty.

The ideal of the American open society centers on
the achievement of total mobility for all its members.
The pluralism that is gradually taking shape under all
these pressures is intended to assure equality of rights
and status to all individuals in the society, to their
samenesses as Americans *and* to their differences as
whatever else they may also happen to be. It is coming
to mean that every individual has unlimited mobility
or freedom of choice not only to become whatever he
wishes to be or can become, but also to retain, however
he might wish it or shape it, his particular identity as a
member of any religious, ethnic, or other subcultural
group which has the vitality to persist and to maintain
itself in its own sphere within the larger community,
and to do this while sharing fully in the common
American identity shared by all. It has taken a long
time, from the beginning until now, for America to
quicken its pace toward this goal. The American actu-

ality naturally falls far short of it, shorter for all non-
whites still than for whites, shorter for Jews than for
non-Jews, much shorter as yet for Negroes than for
Jews. But it falls far less short in every one of these
cases than it fell twenty, ten, even five years ago. Anti-
Catholicism, for example, has become almost an
anachronism in American life within these few years.
Movement in this direction is now constant, the turmoil of the country a function of its present effort to
become more of what it has always claimed to be. No
one can state categorically that this course is irreversi-
ble; great blocks stand in America's way, great drags on
its own ability to renovate itself internally or to wield
effectively the world power that has been thrust upon
it. Even without the ever-present danger of a new
world cataclysm that would bring all this down,
America's own capacity to defeat its own best purposes
remains formidable. But it is not necessary to blink at
the ugly or dangerous realities that persist in American
life to state as a plain fact that no other society on earth
is moving at any comparable pace toward any comparable goal.

The promise of the open society is the American
uniqueness, the American hope, the American offer.
There are pockets and places in Europe—and perhaps
elsewhere—where human beings of different kinds and
professions can coexist in some humanely tolerable
manner. But there is nothing in Europe—or for that
matter in Asia or Africa right now—that resembles the

hope of the American open society, nothing certainly in the possession of any European nationality that offers the Jew what is open to him now in America: the chance to be Jewish *and* American without hyphen or contradiction separating the two identities, to be *Jewish* in whatever way his own genius dictates while sharing as an *American* in the making of a larger, more humane human society. It is the presence of this alternative, something new in the history of the Jews, that marks the difference between Europeans and Americans who have gone to Israel to seek their fulfillment as Jews in the re-created Jewish state. This is where the American pull comes from; this is why so many Americans in Israel find their choices so difficult to make. From the smallness of Israel, the American is pulled back by the bigness of America, by what one early student-immigrant called America's offer of "fulfillment on a continental stage."* He is pulled from Israel's chosen limitedness by America's chosen diversity. He is pulled back from the small cluster of alternatives that life in Israel offers him as the boundaries of his personal existence to the wide breadth of choice —personal, religious, political, social—that lies before every American or, if not yet before *every* American, certainly now more and more before every Jewish American.

There are no doubt some American Jews in Israel

* Quoted by Ernest Stock, *loc. cit.*

who are beyond these pulls, either because of some unique circumstances of their own or because they are totally committed to some other political or religious orientation that would build Israel in some other image. More numerous are the Americans who readily declare their powerful attachment to American values but who have given priority to their Jewishness and interpreted this to mean a full and unqualified commitment to take part in creating the new nation of Jews. This American transmutes the pull of his Americanism into an effort to build these values into the Israel he wants to help create. Like the American devoted to the building of an open society in America, he has to rely on faith and the strength of his conviction to help him confront all the obstacles that appear in his path. But on the American Jew in Israel who has not been able to cast his die quite so far, these pulls lie like tight reins. If they do not draw him all the way back to America, they do keep him from breaking out of that semi-limbo in which he remains suspended between his two identities even while he stays on in Israel and bequeaths the solution of his problem to his children.

Index

Agranat, Simon, 51

Aleichem, Sholem, 138–139

Algerians, 58, 63

Aliya Beth, 81–82

America, open society in, 60–61, 119–120, 130, 233–246

American citizenship, 20, 21, 47, 67, 68; dilemma over choice, 164–246; and government service, 179–181, 190; laws on, 173; and military service, 173–179; and voting, 181–185; renunciation of, 191–192, 197; reasons for retaining, 210–227. *See also* Israeli citizenship. *See* Prefatory Note for U.S. Supreme Court 1967 decision

American identity, 41, 60–61, 106–107, 116, 131; religious attitude in, 150–151; uniqueness of, 233–246

American immigrants, 44–49; reasons for migration, 70–91. *See also* American Jews in Israel

American Israelis: attitudes toward noncitizens, 227–233

American Jews in Israel: numbers, 42–53; children of, 43–44, 224–226; in agriculture, 49–50; in cities, 49–50; in private business, 50–51; in government jobs, 51–52; reasons for migration, 70–91; problems of living, 92–103; satisfactions of, 104 ff.; prejudices against, 113–116; problems of being "Jews," 123–164; and religion, 143–164; dilemma over becoming "Israelis," 164–246. *See also* American citizenship; American

American Jews in Israel (*Cont.*) identity; Jewish identity; Israeli citizenship

American Negroes in West Africa, 15–18, 106, 108

American Society for African Culture, 40

American students in Israel, 114–115, 140–141

"Anglo-Balt kibbutz," 59

"Anglo-Saxon," 27, 53, 54–69, 94, 110, 117, 157, 194, 223

"Anglo-Saxon Shikun," 54–55

Anti-Semitism, 72, 107, 111, 132, 137, 241. *See also* "Jewish question"

Antonovsky, Aaron, 148 n.

Arabs, 1948 war against, 47, 81–82, 142, 167, 174, 180, 196; 1956, 216. *See* Prefatory Note for 1967

Arendt, Hannah, 27

Ashkenazi Jews, 64, 118. *See also* Non-European Jews; Sephardi Jews

Association of Americans and Canadians in Israel, 36–37, 42 n., 45, 47, 48, 55, 61, 65, 67, 94, 98, 100, 108, 156, 166 n., 185–188, 203

Association of Latin American Settlers, 63

Association of Settlers from China, 64

Association of Survivors of Belsen, 63

Association of Survivors of Concentration Camps of Greek Origin, 63

Australians, 53, 60, 110. *See also* "Anglo-Saxon"

Badi, Joseph, 126 n.

"Balts," 59

Bar Kochba, 136

Bavel, 63

Ben-Gurion, David, 123, 125, 139

Bible, 65, 123, 149, 162, 163, 164, 195, 200

B'nei Israel, 149

Breslau, David, 42 n., 166 n.

"British" identity, 60

British mandate, 51

British settlers, 36, 53, 57, 110, 173. *See also* "Anglo-Saxon"

British Settlers Association, 59, 61, 172, 173 n.

Brother Daniel, 126–127

Bureaucracy in Israel, 94, 99–102

Canadians in Israel, 42, 53, 60, 109, 158

"Central European" association, 63

Citizenship, dual, 21. *See also* American citizenship; Israeli citizenship; Prefatory Note

Civil marriage. *See* Religion; Religious authorities

Color, 118–120. *See also* Group identity; "Oriental" Jews

Congregations, non-Orthodox, 148, 157, 159. *See also* Religion; Religious authorities

Conservative Judaism. *See* Religion; Religious authorities

Davis, John A., 40

Diaspora, 68, 147, 163, 205

Diaspora Jews, 51; Israeli view of, 135–144

Dreyfus affair, 241

Eastern European Jews, 45, 46, 51, 60, 74, 136, 155, 162, 172, 201, 241

Eastern Jews. *See* Non-European Jews

Egypt, 172

Egyptians, 58

Eichmann trial, 84

Ein Hashofet, 77

Eisenstein, Ira, 116 n., 154, 155 n.

Eitani, Rita, 128

Elath, 49

England, 53, 59, 60, 94. *See also* "British" identity; British mandate; British settlers; British Settlers Association

English language. *See* Language, problems of

Erikson, Erik, 23

European Jews: outlook compared to Americans, 233–246

Fiddler on the Roof, 138–139

First World War, 44, 75

"Franks," 64

Galanter, Marc, 127 n.

Garvey movement, 18

Gaza strip, 49, 196

German Jews in Israel, 58, 59, 167, 224. *See also* Germany; Hitler; Nazis

Germany, 64, 128, 140, 224, 241

Great Pacific War, 22

Group identity: and political change, 15–41; elements of, 22–35; function of, 23–25; name, 26–27; nation, 27–29; color and physical characteristics, 29–31; race, 29–31; history and origins, 31–32; of Jews in America, 73; crisis of, 129, 131. *See also* National identity

Habonim, 76, 214

Hashomer Hatzair, 76

Hebrew, 43, 62, 64, 65, 67, 68, 82, 95, 99, 137, 138, 164, 185, 186, 197, 203, 225. *See also* Language, problems of

Hebrew University, 51, 54, 121, 140–141, 145

Herman, Simon, 140–141, 140 n.

Herzlia, 56

History and origins. *See* Group identity

Hitachdut Olei America Canada, 65

Hitachdut Olei Germania, 58

Hitler, 34, 46, 58, 60, 79, 81, 84, 89, 111, 130, 140, 142. *See also* Germany; Nazis

Housing, 55, 97–99, 204. *See also* Problems of living in Israel

Indian Jews, 149

Interviews, described, 35–37

Iraq, 63, 172

"Israeli," meaning of, 27, 118, 135 ff., 140–143

Israeli bureaucracy, 115

Israeli citizens, estimated numbers of Americans who have become, 166

Israeli citizenship: dilemma for Americans, 164–246; and military service, 176–179; and government service, 179–181, 190; and voting, 181–185; acceptance of, 192–201; reasons for not accepting, 210–227

Israeli identity cards, 189 ff.

"Jew," Israeli view of, 27, 135 ff. *See also* Jewish identity

Jewish Agency, 36, 57, 97, 98, 100, 103, 168, 187

Jewish Brigade, 174

"Jewish consciousness," 137, 163

Jewish identity, 28, 35, 39, 41, 106 ff., 130, 233 ff.; role of history in, 31; of Jews in America, 73; nation as core, 147; of Indian Jews, 149

Jewish Legion, 75

"Jewish life," 62, 86, 90–91, 104 ff., 143, 152

"Jewish question," 85–91, 131–132

"Jewishness," 35, 82, 85, 86, 118, 123–164, 130, 140, 156, 164, 204, 240

"Jews," definition of, 123–164; attributes of, 140–143

Jobs, 96, 204. *See also* Problems of living in Israel

Jordan, 49, 50

Joseph, Dov, 51

Judaism: in Israel, 122 ff., 200. *See also* Religion; Religious authorities

Kahn, Sholom, 121, 121 n., 224 n.

Kaplan, Meier, 108–109

Kaye, Danny, 139

Kerem, Moshe, 228

Kfar Shmaryahu, 158

Kibbutzim, Americans and, 36, 40, 48, 59, 68, 76, 77, 79, 84, 86, 92, 93, 107, 112, 143, 151, 153, 162, 198, 204; child-rearing practices, 116; religion, 154; and military service, 178; and voting, 182–185; and citizenship, 194

Korean War, 85, 175

"Kurdi," 64

Landsmannschaft organizations, 61–65

Language, problems of, 43–44, 62, 95, 96, 99, 138, 204, 206, 225. *See also* Hebrew

Lapide, P. E., 48 n., 82 n., 169 n.

Latin American Jews in Israel, 63, 172

Law of Return, 66, 66 n., 67, 126, 128, 168

League Against Religious Coercion, 149. *See also* Religion; Religious authorities

Lehrman, Hal, 95 n.

Lev, Yehuda, 55 n.

"Litvaks," 59

Maghreb, 64

Mahal, 81–82

Mapai, 36, 126 n., 147, 182

Mapam, 36, 126 n., 147, 182, 215

Meir, Golda, 45, 51

Military service. *See* American citizenship; Israeli citizenship

Mizrachi, 147

Moroccans, 58, 63, 64, 232. *See also* Non-European Jews

Moshavim, 48

Namali, Shalom, 106 n.

Name, 54–69, 68; national labels acquired in Israel, 57–60. *See also* Group identity

Nation. *See* Group identity

National identity, 27–29, 57–60. *See also* Group identity; Nationality

Nationality, 20, 27, 28, 41, 57–60, 58, 164, 193, 240, 245

Nationality groups, 61–65

Naturei Karta, 146, 218

Nazis, 58, 60, 64, 79, 81, 84, 128. *See also* Germany; Hitler

Negroes, 15–18, 21, 39, 40, 107, 119, 242

New Zealanders, 61

Non-European Jews, 41, 63–64, 117–121, 144, 237. *See also* Moroccans; North Africa

North Africa, 30, 63, 111, 172. *See also* Landsmannschaft organizations; Non-European Jews

Olei, meaning of, 65–66

"Oriental Jews." *See* Non-European Jews

Orthodox, 124 ff., 146, 148. *See also* Religion; Religious authorities; Ultra-orthodox Jews

Orthodox Rabbinical Council of America, 157 n.

Palestine, 44, 45, 58, 74, 75, 167, 195, 196

Patterson, Charles J., 17

Permanent resident status, 67, 166–169, 208

Poland, 76, 82, 150

Poles, 58

Problems of living in Israel, 92–103; cost of living, 96; jobs, 96; housing, 97–99. *See also* Bureaucracy in Is-real; Language, problems of

Rabbinical establishment, 124 ff.

Rabbis, 40, 186; American, 156–161; Conservative, 123, 157 n.; Reform, 123, 157 n.

Race. *See* Group identity; Non-European Jews

Reform Judaism. *See* Religion; Religious authorities

Religion, 123–164; and state, 125 ff., 125 n.; Americans and, 143–164; Israeli attitudes on, 148

Religious authorities, 124 ff.; and definition of "Jew," 125–129; and state rela-tions, 125 n.; religious mi-norities, 151; problems of marriage, 124, 149, 151, 153–154, 186

Rosenfeld, Alvin, 95 n.

Rumania, 58, 77, 150

Sanders, Ronald, 95 n., 126 n., 236

Sartre, Jean-Paul, 131–136

Second World War, 45, 167, 201

"Senior residents," 52–53, 201–203

Sephardi Jews, 64, 118. *See also* Non-European Jews

Simon, Ernst, 144 n.

South Africa, 53, 60, 94, 172–173

South African Jews in Israel, 30, 36, 110, 173

South African Zionist Federa-tion, 61, 173

Soviet Union, 150

Standard of living, 96. *See also* Problems of living in Israel

Stern, Ilana, 127 n.

Stock, Ernest, 121 n., 235, 245 n.

Suez crisis, 1956, 216

Supreme Court of Israel, 125, 158

Syria, 49

Talmon, J. L., 129 n., 145
Talmud, 124
"Temporary resident" status, 67, 166–169, 204

Ultra-orthodox Jews, 46, 146. *See also* Orthodox; Religion; Religious authorities
United States. *See* America, open society in; American citizenship; American identity; American immigrants; American Israelis; American Jews in Israel; American Negroes in West Africa; American Society for African Culture; American students in Israel
United States Supreme Court, 174–175, 190–191. *See also* Prefatory Note
Urban dwellers, 49–50; problems of living, 93 ff., 108, 167, 182, 187

Walter-McCarran Act, 1952, 172–173

Weiner, Herbert, 126, 145 n., 162
Whartman, Eliezer, 95 n.

"Yeckes," 58, 59 n.
Yemen, 172
Yeshiva University, 197
Yiddish, 64, 82, 137, 138, 201, 203. *See also* Hebrew; Language in Israel
Yiddishkeit, 138, 139
Yordim, 66, 66 n.

Zionism, 84, 108, 241
Zionist Labor Organization, 76
Zionist Organization of America, 157 n.
Zionist youth groups, 92, 94, 142, 147, 175, 194, 204
Zionists, 45, 65, 66, 82, 83, 84, 116, 147, 150, 154, 167, 205; early backgrounds, 74–80; youth groups, 74–80